Long Live
the Family Business!

Long Live the Family Business!

THE POWER OF FAMILY MEETINGS

AND OTHER PRACTICAL TRANSITION STRATEGIES

TO HELP YOUR BUSINESS THRIVE

LES BANWART

BIG SNOWY
Media

Big Snowy Media, 209 E. Liberty Drive, Wheaton, IL 60187

Big Snowy Media edition published 2020

Library of Congress Cataloging-in-Publication Data

Long Live the Family Business! (Big Snowy Media)

Includes index.

1. Business strategy—United States. 2. Leadership.

I. Title

ISBN 978-0-578-78303-1

Dedicated to all entrepreneurs
who are thinking about or
have established their own business.

CONTENTS

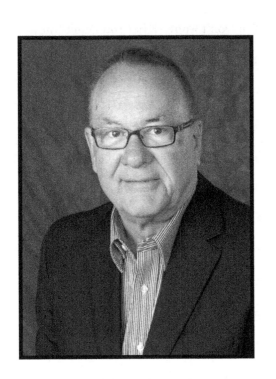

M y intention in writing this book is that you treat it as one of your advisers when planning for the transition of your company from one generation to the next.

It applies mainly to first, second, and third generation family and closely-held companies, and is a distillation of knowledge I have accumulated from listening to and consulting with family and closely-held businesses for over forty years. I believe it will help you develop and implement a transition strategy to ensure your business and your family thrive. The advice I give can also help you improve the operations of your business for the betterment of the owners and employees.

This advice is practical, not theoretical. It's what owners need to hear, although not always what they want to hear.

During my twenty-five years with Arthur Andersen, I dealt solely with family-owned and closely-held companies. I saw the struggles between the owners and succeeding generations as they faced transition planning.

As a tax partner, I began to facilitate family meetings, which is the first step in helping business owners through a transition. Upon retiring from Arthur Andersen in 1997, I started a family office and a family council at the request of one of my former clients as they prepared to sell their company. When they sold the company for more than a billion dollars, I helped them establish Aileron, a not-for-profit entrepreneurial campus, to teach professional management to business owners. While teaching classes on transition planning at Aileron, I enjoyed helping these owners understand the transition process while also learning from them about the issues they faced in their day-to-day operations. After retiring from the family office, as well as my position of Vice-Chair of Aileron, I started my own business, Banwart Strategies, LLC. I have been currently consulting with a variety of clients on transition issues, as well as other operational concerns. I also speak at seminars and entrepreneurial classes at universities. The variety of interaction with clients and students is energizing!

Over the years I have watched owners create hardship for their companies and families because they are unaware of, or forget, or choose to ignore these basic concepts of building a business: plan for the future, communicate with the family, know when to let go, and, above all, *listen.* I have also seen businesses completely turn around when owners pay attention to these basic concepts. A business can flourish, lasting through generations, when grounded in these fundamentals.

There are many books on transitioning that discuss the problems, without providing any answers. Their authors complicate the idea of transition, and withhold the answers in hope of getting new clients.

This book gives answers and provides alternatives to consider as you plan your transition. While the concepts in this book are not difficult, they are not easy to put into practice, mostly because they don't come naturally or intuitively to business owners focused on operations, production, and customer satisfaction. They require a dedicated effort.

I encourage you to absorb and apply my practical advice. I believe it will help you do the hard and necessary things to successfully transition your business.

Each of these chapters could be a book in itself, and unnecessarily long! I want this book to be a quick resource to help you visualize how you might approach a transition plan. I give practical examples of what you need to do to develop your own plan for your successful family or closely-held business.

I deeply admire owners of family-held businesses for numerous reasons: putting their own money at risk, which differentiates them from public companies; building our economy by employing millions; and creating most of the new jobs in our country, thus strengthening our nation. I have gotten to know many owners and their families and am grateful for their dedication, hard work, and values of caring, fairness, and loyalty in achieving their families' dreams.

I hope this book will make a positive impact on your family, as well as in transitioning your business.

CHAPTER 1

You Don't Know What You Don't Know

had just opened my Q&A during my seminar on transition strategies for a group of entrepreneurs when someone shouted from the back of the room, "The last thing I need is a consultant like you telling me how to run my business!"

"I'm not telling you how to run your business," I replied. "I'm providing alternatives to help you think differently about how you run your business and what your business might become." I continued, "Perhaps there are a few things you haven't thought about. Maybe you need strategic planning, or advice in transitioning your company, or steps to follow in setting up an outside board. If you don't know about these issues, how can you say you don't need them?"

You don't know what you don't know. This is a double-edged statement. On the one hand, you're not responsible for what you don't know. On the other hand, when you are faced with new situations you have the responsibility to learn what you don't know.

It's also a very practical statement. If you've never transitioned your business how would you know what to do? Most entrepreneurs who build a business from the ground up don't know how to build it out into succeeding generations. Ironically, family and closely-held businesses owners don't know how to transition their businesses but they do know how to run them, and they believe it's all they need to know.

Be Open to Change

Ask business owners about their businesses—their humble beginnings and how they have built their enterprises—and you will hear how they take pride in sharing their stories. Ask them where their businesses will be in ten to fifteen years and watch them struggle for words. Family business owners rarely talk about what's going to happen to the business because they often don't understand how to plan for it. They've never done it before, and the unknown scares them. They stick to what they know, which is how to build a successful company by making a good product, providing services, and treating their employees and customers with respect and dignity. Instead of preparing a transition plan for the future, they rely on their past successes. Why change the formula? Keeping a good thing going is easier than changing a good thing.

Change could bring a risk of loss, which is a more powerful motivator than the potential for gain. It is why the predictable is preferred to the uncertain. However, risk is inherent to business, and business growth must incorporate both the potential reward and the uncertainty of risk. Successful companies are

III

Know your own mind
well enough to mistrust it.

IIIIIIIIIIIIIIIIIIIIIIIIIIIIIIIIIIIIIIIIIII

highly responsive to competition, culture, technology, and all other forms of disruption. They have an intense hunger for taking action, coupled with a high tolerance for risk. These companies are open to change.

Change Is Hard

The first requirement for changing your business is to change the way you think about your business. As I told the entrepreneurs in the seminar, the key concept is to think differently. You must constantly look at how you might operate your business in a different way. This means a change in mindset, which is especially hard. After all, you have learned to trust your mind to get you to where you are right now. Maybe that's why you're reading this book. You don't like where you are right now.

Know your own mind well enough to mistrust it. This maxim underlies all the advice I have given to family business owners over the years. You don't always make the best choices and good decisions. Because your judgement is biased your mind can easily be led astray. For proof of this, look at any optical illusion. What you see is not what's there, even though your mind is telling you to trust what you see. This does not mean something is wrong with you. It's simply the way the human mind works. It can be led astray. What's important is for you to recognize you can't always trust your mind.

Much of this book is about how to correct or prevent common mistakes in running a business. As I have said, many of these mistakes stem from lack of knowledge. That's not your fault, but it does oblige you to find out what you don't know. If you're aware of the alternatives but unreceptive, this may hurt your family, and your business. Bad decisions are directly the result of acting out of avoidance or lack of knowledge.

Building and transitioning a family-owned or closely-held company to the second and third generations is an especially challenging arena for decision making. New businesses have a failure rate of 66% during the first ten years.[1] Much of this can be attributed to the inherent risks of running a business, which may include such obstacles as: no market need, not enough capital, competition, pricing, and hiring practices. Sometimes, though, business failure is due to avoidable mistakes, which are compounded by these risks. Facing these obstacles requires being open to change.

Hard but Necessary

To successfully transition your business, you will need to make hard but necessary decisions throughout every phase of growth. These decisions reflect a willingness to think differently about your business. In this book I address fundamental practices which are critical to the long-term health of your

---

1 According to the Bureau of Labor Statistics, 30% in the first two years of being open, 50% during the first five years, and 66% during the first ten.

|||||||||||||||||||||||||||||||||||||||||||||||

When you hear advice you don't want to hear, please take notes and read those notes two or three days later.

|||||||||||||||||||||||||||||||||||||||||||||||

business. They are not complex. They are not theoretical. They do not require advanced degrees to understand them. They are practical but not easy. The acronym KISS, "Keep It Simple, Stupid," is well known and often used, partly because we tend to complicate our lives by failing to apply the basics. The difficult part is initiating those basic practices.

Basic practices are hard to put in place because they run up against systemic biases in the way we think and act, biases which are built into our nature. We have natural tendencies to talk before we listen, to be unrealistically optimistic about our performance, to go along with the status quo, and to avoid change or any kind of loss.

We also inadvertently deceive ourselves and we foolishly cut corners. These are part of a long list of human behaviors leading to mistakes which can undermine a business. The business practices in this book counter these tendencies and will help you avoid or correct the mistakes they can cause. More importantly, these best practices can improve the way you do business and how you plan your transition to the next generation.

Be Advised

I will say it again. "Don't always trust your mind." Sometimes it tells you to choose the wrong actions. When you are making strategic decisions for the business look for trusted advisers and run any questions by them. Be careful here. Take time to find good advisers. You'll know they are good by the way they listen. A listening adviser tests your thinking. If you realize you've made mistakes, advisers can help you trace them back to poor decisions and understand why you made them. They can then offer ideas for changes in your business culture to prevent repeating the same mistakes.

Successful entrepreneurs have learned to listen and to realize good advice can come from many difference sources. They have received intense feedback from real life situations, not from theories in a textbook. James Dyson, the inventor of the cyclone vacuum, went through 5,127 prototypes to create a machine that had no bag and no loss of suction. He learned by paying attention and continually making changes based on the feedback he received.

Paying attention and making changes based on feedback is the essence of listening. Listening is a simple concept, though often difficult to put into practice. It entails listening to advisers who are not afraid to confront you with reality. They will tell you the truth about what they are thinking, even if it is something you don't want to hear.

I strongly recommend when you hear advice you don't want to hear, please take notes and read those notes two or three days later. I guarantee you will feel differently about the advice.

Listening is fundamental to all the practices I describe in this book. They are practical, and for the most part simple, but require discipline and effort. You can't do them alone. You will need to ask for help from trusted advisers and be willing to listen to them. In an upcoming chapter I thoroughly address the value of good advice.

CHAPTER 2

The Power of a Family Meeting

I can't stress enough the importance of this chapter on family meetings. Without these meetings all the issues surfacing during the transition will more than likely never be resolved. Without all adult family members at the meeting, a transition plan will most likely fail. Resolving transition issues is not up to one person or a small number of family members. A successful transition must involve the entire family at a meeting with a facilitator who will make sure all issues are brought to everyone's attention and fully discussed.

It was my introductory meeting with the first-generation husband and wife owners of a family business, whose three sons helped run the company.

"For the initial step," I said, "let's talk with all your children and their spouses."

"But my daughters-in-law really dislike me," the wife said.

When I asked her why, she said she didn't know.

"Then we need to find out," I said, because this issue was affecting how the sons were working together and running the company.

"Finding out" is exactly why I insist on a family meeting, where the purpose is to get all the issues on the table. A good transition plan must deal with all the real issues, whether personal or business, which might help or hinder the transition from one generation to the next. The only way to get to the real issues is through a process of discovery. As I was to find out, the daughters-in-law were indeed hostile to their mother-in-law, but discovering the reason why they were angry would make all the difference to the business and to the family.

When I'm asked to help plan the transition for a family business, the focus is on the inner workings and relationships of the family. I conduct a two-step discovery process. The first step is confidential interviews with each individual family member, which sets the stage for the second step, a family meeting with all family members present. This meeting almost always includes spouses of the family members, as well. Critically valuable insights can come from a person who is not directly involved with the company but has intimate knowledge of the person who is. I highly recommend in-laws be involved in all family meetings.

In my interviews with the daughters-in-law, each of them told me, "Our mother-in-law is trying to control us and our children, and we're not going to let her do it."

"How does she control you?" I asked one of them.

"She sends us e-mails to ask that we send our children to spend time with her."

‖‖‖‖‖‖‖‖‖‖‖‖‖‖‖‖‖‖‖‖‖‖‖‖‖‖‖‖‖‖

I highly recommend in-laws be involved in all family meetings.

‖‖‖‖‖‖‖‖‖‖‖‖‖‖‖‖‖‖‖‖‖‖‖‖‖‖‖‖‖‖

"What's wrong with that?"

"We know her. We know what's she's doing," she said.

"And how do you know?" I asked.

These were the early days of email before anyone had learned to proceed with caution when typing an electronic message, and before there were emojis to insert into the communication what emails (or texts) leave out: body language. Even now, though, emails and messages can be misinterpreted. When the intent of the communication isn't clear, we almost always assume the worst, which is what the daughters-in-law had done.

Before conducting all the interviews, I always promise confidentiality. I had both sides of the story, but not the full story. It took a family meeting to get to the truth. When we gathered around the table I asked the most vocal of the daughters-in-law, "Would you be willing to tell everyone here what you told me?" I had cleared this with her before the meeting.

After she had finished, her mother-in-law burst into tears. "All I want is to see my grandkids."

There was silence. And then from one of the daughters-in-law, "That's it? That's all you wanted?"

"I'm their grandmother. What else could I possibly want?"

As with many conflicts that can turn into pitched battles, this standoff was based on misunderstanding and one astounding misperception, which all stemmed from failing to communicate. This doesn't seem to be all that big an issue. However, if these types of issues go unresolved they can tear a family apart and, in this case, could have ruined the company.

Some of these seemingly minor issues can go back to child-hood. I dealt with one family with seven children, where two brothers never could find common ground. They constantly argued about how to transition the company.

During my interview with one of those brothers I brought up the conflicts they were having. To my surprise and total dismay, he explained how his older brother always threw sand in his face when they played in the sandbox as children. It was then I learned conflict between adults can carry through starting from a very young age.

We Have to Start Meeting Like This

The email miscommunication and childhood bullying under-score the importance of having a face-to-face family meeting, where everyone gets to speak, and everyone is heard.

Even though family meetings are essential to moving both the business and the family forward, unfortunately they sel-dom take place. There are numerous reasons for this.

Older generations are afraid of delving into problem areas and bringing to the surface issues which can disrupt the equilibrium of both the business and the family. Their mindset is to leave well enough alone. This creates the status quo bias I have mentioned previously. When systems are proceeding normally, it's easy to create a false sense that all is well. The older generations often rely on their experiences, and "go with their gut." These intuitive and decisive judgements can drive the business forward, but they can also be flawed, especially if the oldest generations do not recognize their own mistakes.

This is understandable. People don't typically anticipate their mental errors and correct for them. Instead, they make wrong decisions based on their misconceptions. In addition, the older generation is sometimes dismissive of ideas from the younger generations, ideas which could help the business adapt to an ever changing economic and technological environment. The older generations often want to protect and perpetuate what they have rather than risk bringing up issues that will advance but also could potentially disrupt the company.

The younger generation is inclined to defer to the hopes and dreams which initially led their elders to build the business in the first place. For fear they might disrespect those dreams, the second and third generations frequently stay quiet when they should be speaking up.

The generations simply need to have a conversation, but it's not that simple. Clear, direct, and positive communication to advance the conversation is notoriously difficult. Emotions, biases, and entrenched misconceptions inhibit the "clear the air" conversations necessary for progress.

Because these conversations are hard, families may resort to other types of communication, like the emails described which intensify misunderstandings and can ultimately break a family or a business apart. Perhaps the most common and damaging communication is what I call triangulating, better known as gossiping, which is the triangle. In essence, gossiping is talking *about* a person instead of talking *to* the person. When we are afraid of confrontation, and challenging conversations, we default to gossip, which is conflict avoidance. It can also be considered lazy. Triangulation in navigation can safely guide a ves-

||||||||||||||||||||||||||||||||||||||||||||||||

The first family meeting will yield
the necessary results ONLY
with the help of a facilitator.

||||||||||||||||||||||||||||||||||||||||||||||||

sel, but in relationships it has the opposite effect and can steer an organization onto the rocks.

The best way to break up the gossip triangle is to simply tell people it is vital to talk to each other rather than about each other. This can be difficult to do, especially among family members who know each other so well. When sibling rivalry, perceptions of favoritism, and other family dynamics are factored in, emotions can run high and prevent clear and open communication.

In family meetings, the triangles are all in one room, and a discussion can take place with all the right people in the conversation. While triangulating is lazy, inflammatory, and prompted by fear, effective conversations require courage, hard work, and careful thought. They can be enormously productive and helpful in crafting an effective transition plan. There is no doubt in my mind, however, that the first family meeting will yield the necessary results ONLY with the help of a facilitator.

The Power of a Facilitator

"Get that b_____ away from me."

Her vehemence startled me. We were in a multi-generational family meeting with more than 100 members present, of which the oldest generation were all owners in the family business. They all lived in the same city, but never spoke to each other. This was the first time in thirty years they had gotten together in the same room. The meeting also included cousins, one of whom made the harsh comment.

"I can't stand her," she continued, and proceeded to tell me why.

When she finished, I simply asked, "Why don't you move to the other side of the room?"

"Well, I hadn't thought of that," she said. The solution was simple, but more than that, it was practical. It worked, and the meeting continued.

It was also not an overly ambitious solution. Another consultant might have tried to bring the two hostile parties together, which would have caused chaos, and unnecessarily disrupted—or broken up—the meeting. I have learned to never force reconciliation in a hostile situation. Be pragmatic, not idealistic. Do what you can to de-escalate, then move forward.

This brief exchange also illustrates why an experienced facilitator must run the family meeting. Family meetings can be explosive. A facilitator helps harness that emotional energy so it fuels the conversation instead of blowing up the meeting and driving family members even further away from each other.

Facilitators can also help family members by opening their eyes to how their emotions are blinding them to the solution that's right in front of them, which can be as simple as moving to a seat on the other side of the room.

The root word for facilitator or facilitate is the Latin *facilis*, which means "easy." A facilitator helps ease the communication, by creating a safe environment where hard issues are easier to present and also easier to hear. If family members can listen to each other during the difficult conversations, they will be able to hear the wisdom of a different point of view and stay at the table to discern a way forward for the business.

The facilitator is the key to a successful family meeting. A facilitator's power does not lie in the ability to control the meeting, but to guide it in the right direction. Facilitators do not influence; instead, they help family members confront situations and issues, and they bring up alternatives. They see the big picture and the broad perspective from all the interviews, and help the family consider the long-term outcome. When family members are buffeted by the emotions of the moment, a facilitator creates a neutral environment in which the family can make decisions.

The family members have all the expertise, experience, wisdom, and insight into the business to make those essential decisions. They need an experienced leader to get them through the turbulence. A facilitator does not need to know about the business to help the family discuss the right issues and resolve the problems that surface in the transition planning process.

Thankfully, my suggestion to the angry cousin opened the door to other possibilities for the family. A simple and practical solution got the cousins thinking about how they might change the atmosphere for the better. At the end of the meeting they made a pact that they would not act like their parents, who had quit communicating with each other. They also decided to get together regularly, simply to enjoy each other. The owners eventually sold the company, which was the right decision for the family. When the family can communicate openly, they generally make the right decisions for the business and the family.

iii

When the family can communicate
openly, they generally make the right
decisions for the business and the family.

iiiiiiiiiiiiiiiiiiiiiiiiiiiiiiiiiiiiiiiiiii

I called my longtime mentor, Léon Danco, and told him I felt I failed this family because they ultimately sold their business. He immediately responded: "Les, you did your job because you got them to do *something*! It is not up to you as a facilitator to try to convince the family to keep the business, but to give them the alternatives they need to make the best decisions for the family, which you helped them do."

Individual Interviews

A productive conversation presumes trust. The facilitator's goal is to get all family members to trust each other enough to open up. This will only happen if the facilitator knows each family member well enough to safeguard the process of the family meeting and also ensure that a sometimes-fragile trust is not broken. While facilitators do not know all that takes place in the business, they must learn as much as they can about each family member, including extended family. Personal and confidential interviews accomplish this. At the beginning of each interview I assure each person I will not reveal the source of any issues discussed with me and I will bring up all issues on my own. This builds trust between family members and the facilitator. Going into a family meeting I know most of the issues to help me guide the larger conversation because the issues have emerged in the personal meetings.

This type of interview relies on listening carefully, asking the right questions, and allowing the person time to answer before asking the next question. It's a gradual process of discovery with enough time to address the real issues, which typically don't surface until the second hour of the interview. By then I have established rapport and trust for the family member to talk freely. Often the most revealing information appears almost as an afterthought when we are winding down the meeting.

I once had a conversation with a business owner that continued in spin cycle for over two hours, until he grabbed both arms of his chair, leaned forward, and said, "Les, I don't even have a will!" It had taken him that long to trust me enough and gather the courage to admit he didn't have one. If he had died without a will his business would have been in shambles. We started the process with his attorney as soon as our interview ended.

The thoughts and opinions gathered in the individual meetings are critical to the success of the transition. They can now be discussed in the family meeting, without attributing them to the individual. As I have mentioned, the younger generations often submerge their true feelings, for fear of disappointing the oldest generation. The goal is to get the generations talking to one another, addressing the current reality, instead of relying on assumptions that might be flat-out wrong.

A first-generation business owner told me his story: My son came home for Christmas break during his last year at college. I hugged him and said, 'Well, I finally did it. I sold the company.' I was shocked when he said, "What! I thought I was going to run this company."

"You never told me that!" I said.

"Dad, you never asked me!"

When there is no conversation, assumptions fill the void. When we act on those assumptions the void can become a rift. Critical information that closes the rift can come out in a family meeting when generations open up and express their feelings to each other.

Sometimes children do not want to work in the family business, but are afraid to tell their parents. They might find their parents would be happy to help them pursue their passion, whether it's starting a new business, or working for another company in a different industry. As important as the family business is to first-generation founders, their children's happiness is even more important.

I also have questions directed at top management of the company, if they are included in the interviews. After interviewing all the individuals, I note any common issues which consistently emerged, so I can address them in the family meeting. This provides a certain amount of anonymity while reassuring family members they are not alone. Others may also share their viewpoint.

Time Out

Guiding an intense and emotionally-laden discussion is a difficult task. That's one reason why facilitators employ simple tools. When things get overheated I call a time out, a break for the whole family. It's the equivalent of telling someone who's hyperventilating to stop and take a deep slow breath. The brain needs to take over, regulating the body, and telling it

||||||||||||||||||||||||||||||||||||||||||

When there is no conversation,
assumptions fill the void.
When we act on those assumptions
the void can become a rift.

||||||||||||||||||||||||||||||||||||||||||

to breathe. It's what I did when the woman "requested" that I get her cousin away from her. Stop. Breathe. Think about what you just said. What's the next most helpful thing to do or say?

During a time out, the family member who has sucked the oxygen out of the room can quietly reconsider the outburst. Usually there's an apology and a clarification. Often the point is valid, and is important to the conversation. It simply needs to be stated without the emotional smokescreen.

Not only an outburst calls for a time out. Sometimes it's a sidebar discussion two family members are holding. When I see a sidebar, I stop the meeting and ask them to share. "If it's important enough to warrant a private conversation while others are talking, the rest of the family needs to hear it," I say. If the sidebar participants answer, "We're not sure this is the place to bring it up," I assure them, "This is absolutely the place to bring it up. All the issues need to be on the table."

Make an Issue of It

In life we are often instructed to "let it go," to not "make an issue of it." While this is sometimes good advice—relationships should rise above pettiness—I have found the opposite advice

||||||||||||||||||||||||||||||||||||||||||

When families talk openly
and candidly in a safe environment,
the result is often astounding.

||||||||||||||||||||||||||||||||||||||||||

to be very helpful in most family businesses. Bring the issues to the surface so the family can address them together. Families tend to submerge problems, which makes them even bigger. When problems aren't discussed, rifts grow and fault lines develop until eventually there is an earthquake. Problems go unaddressed, and opportunities go by the wayside because the younger family members don't voice them.

My goal is to get families talking about transition. When families talk openly and candidly in a safe environment, the result is often astounding. Relationships are restored, issues are resolved, and a transition plan can be solidified.

I opened this chapter with a story about a giant rift between a mother-in-law and her daughters-in-law. As the meeting ended, I said, "Here's what I want you to do. First, stop using email for emotional issues. Pick up the phone. Second, agree to have dinner tonight, all of you, and make sure all the grandkids are there." Two days later the father called me. "Les, you helped us save our family as well as the company!"

His response shows why a seemingly simplistic approach can have such powerful results. These practical solutions help untangle complicated family issues so they can be resolved.

CHAPTER 3

Plan While You Still Can

I t was a generous transaction.

An owner sold his business to his son at a forty percent discount, which represented an enormous sum of money at the time.

For a family business, it was also a thoughtless transaction because the owner had four sons. When I asked him about his other sons, he said, "They have their own businesses. They will make it on their own."

Five years later the son who bought the business called me. "Les, I need your help. My father's succession plan has created all kinds of problems between my brothers and me. They are jealous, and they resent me for our dad's decision that gave me the advantage."

He then added, "Let's start talking now about a transition plan for my children."

Fortunately, the son had the foresight his father didn't have, and did what his father didn't do. He put a transition plan in place that would benefit the entire family, the employees, and ultimately the business. His father's succession plan, on the other hand, was simply a one-time transaction without considering the long-term impact on the family, as well as the business.

I define transition as a step-by-step plan for ongoing leadership of a company beyond its current generation. What I often encounter is a reluctance to put such a plan in place.

A Deathly Fear

Most business owners don't loosen their grip until circumstances force their hand. Not wanting to let go affects *how* they let go. Because they don't have a long-term mindset and a corresponding long-term plan, the succession can be as sudden and swift as death or disability, and often causes the failure of the business.

Thinking of death is an apt analogy, because it is quite literally one of the biggest reasons why family business owners do not put a plan in place. They are afraid of dying. To them a succession plan sounds like the end.

The fear of death is not unusual, so it's understandable if a succession plan is associated with dying, the oldest generations will avoid it. The business is not just their baby, it's their life, and its loss represents a kind of death. Conversely, when they are experiencing the flush of business success, owners might think they and their businesses will go on forever. Often their only thought is to keep doing what they've always done, expecting the same results. Consequently, they don't plan for succeeding generations.

Accompanying the fear of dying is the fear of estate plan-

There have been many efficient tax plans put in place with total disregard to the long-term effect on the family.

ning. Business owners dread it. When they hear "succession plan," many owners don't think about the future of the business, but its end. Their minds go immediately to inheritance and tax planning. Their lawyers and accountants will encourage them to prioritize estate planning, but that's putting the cart before the horse. You may find out it's not the best tax plan. This is not uncommon. There have been many efficient tax plans put in place with total disregard to the long-term effect on the family. Always do what's right for the family. Estate planning should happen only after a transition plan is in place. A family needs to figure out the future of the business first, and then give their attorneys and accountants one clear instruction: "Here's what we decided to do as a family. Don't screw it up. Design the plan to fit our needs."

That might sound harsh but I wish someone had said exactly that to me. As a former tax planner with Arthur Andersen, I put together many tax plans. I soon realized the plans were more about saving taxes than helping the family. They were good plans as far as they went, but they didn't go far enough. I wasn't considering where the family business might be in ten to fifteen years. I learned to think differently. A transition plan takes into consideration values other than making and saving money.

Succession vs. Transition: What's the Difference?

Planning is, in essence, long-term thinking. Entrepreneurs are natural risk takers and innovators, but the ones who succeed are also planners who have a vision for where they are going and the strategic plan to get there. I have found owners tend to be very aware of the short-term and ignore the long-term, putting their businesses in jeopardy. Short-term thinking repeated again and again doesn't lead to long-term thinking.

To grow a small family business into a multi-generational business takes long-term planning which a sudden succession simply cannot accomplish.

Throughout this book, I will use the word *transition* instead of *succession*. When a family-owned business makes a smooth hand-off to the next generation of leadership, it is a transition, not a single moment in time. The transition has happened gradually, though surely, over a span of time because of long-term thinking. It ensures not only the business survives but also that the family thrives into the next generation.

As I noted in the previous chapter, it's difficult to change our actions without first changing our minds. That's why I advise business owners to think differently about the future of their businesses, to change their mindsets from succession to transition. It's vital to understand the differences between the two:

• **Transition is continuation. Succession is replacement.** To business owners, succession means they're being replaced. One day they're in, the next day they're out, suddenly separated from a primary source of purpose in their lives. Transition

When it comes to complex matters,
emotionally-driven decisions
are seldom good decisions.

focuses on continuation by laying the groundwork for a long-term plan which should continue to involve the owner.

• **Transition is long-term planning. Succession is more immediate.** Succession happens all at one time and one place, and often leaves the family reeling, wondering, "What do we do with this monster?" It happens to the family, whether they like it or not, whether they are all aware of it or not. Transition is relational. It happens gradually, though surely, with the family members involved in the process. A transition plan must have buy-in from all family members. Even if there is not complete agreement on the process, everyone is committed to the plan. In this way, a transition plan communicates that you care for the entire family, and have the family's best interest in mind, as well as the future of the business.

• **Transition anticipates something new. Succession spells the end.** Succession is an abrupt transfer of ownership dominated by the reality that the older generation is gone, creating a void in leadership and direction. Transition focuses on what the family wants to do with the business long before the loss of the older generation. It is proactive rather than reactive. Business owners are also able to transition themselves into new areas and interests while still being involved in the

||||||||||||||||||||||||||||||||||||||||||||||||

A transition plan must have a buy-in
from all family members.

||||||||||||||||||||||||||||||||||||||||||||||||

business if they choose. They realize they can develop different sides of themselves, something they didn't have time to do when they were building and running their businesses.

• **Transition is not emotionally-driven. Succession is charged with emotion.** We don't like loss of any kind, and the loss of a parent who has also run the family business can be even more traumatic. If no transition plan is already in place a family must decide under duress what to do with the business. When it comes to complex matters, emotionally-driven decisions are seldom good decisions.

A transition plan has taken the absence of the owner into account. More importantly, the plan usually goes into effect while the owner is still alive. The family has control of the gradual process of letting go because they have set up the business to succeed without direct involvement of the older generation.

That's A Plan

How many steps does a transition plan take? As many as necessary.

The first step, however, is always the same, and it's the most important step: have a family meeting.

Sometimes, the first step is the only step needed.

I had arranged a first meeting with a potential client, a father and daughter, on a no-fee basis. I do this at all my first meetings simply to see if we can work together.

As they sat down, the father shook his head, "Les, we don't know what to do with the company."

"Who's been working in the company?" I asked.

"My daughter," said the father. "I've got one son, and he doesn't want to have anything to do with it. But if I give it to my daughter, I'm sure he'll take a sudden interest."

"Why don't you sell it to your daughter over multiple years?" I offered. "She can use profits from your company and pay your note down. That's a plan."

He propelled himself out of his chair. "That's it! That's the answer! I had never thought about selling it to her. I couldn't get past the idea of giving it to her, which would have created its own problems."

"Well then, there's your plan," I said. "And it didn't cost you a penny." That meeting, by the way, was the shortest one I ever had.

CHAPTER 4

Strategic Planning

G row or die. These are the only options for a family business. The only way to survive is to grow. The only way to grow is to have a vision and a plan.

My colleague and I were in a planning meeting with a company's top management, all of whom thought we were dreaming. The company had been at twenty million in sales annually for the past several years, and we had just given them one goal: to be at sixty million in sales within five years.

"Are you kidding?" they chorused, and began to throw objections at us. "We don't have the sales people."

"We would need new locations."

"Our owners don't want to spend the money."

"Stop!" we said. "All we're hearing are obstacles. We want to hear what it's going to take to get there."

"Impossible," said the VP of Operations. "One of our competitors is crushing us."

"Why don't you look at it as an opportunity?" we responded. "Have you thought about working with your competitor?"

"That's the last thing we would consider."

We persisted. "They might want YOU to help THEM. Otherwise they, or another company, will most certainly crush you. Come back to the next meeting and tell us how you're going to get to sixty million. Don't worry about the roadblocks."

In two months they returned, brimming with optimism, as well as a sales increase of fifteen million to thirty-five million. They had passed the thought process down to their subordinates who immediately seized the idea and suggested to their competitor that they help each other. The collaboration spawned new ideas for the use of their product which contributed to the growth of both companies.

Vision Is the Driver

Vision drives a company forward. It is both optimistic and opportunistic. Vision is also seeing a company's potential and projecting it into the future. It's where they want to be. By challenging the company to triple their sales, we cast a vision which compelled them to think beyond their current reality and envision a new one. Our challenge became their vision for a strategic plan.

Tripling revenue in five years was an aggressive vision. Initially, all the managers could see were the problems directly in front of them, not the potential solutions that were also there. They were boxed in, dominated by group think, and not generating any fresh ideas. They needed some out-of-the-box thinking. When we studied their product, we knew it had potential to be repurposed for other industries.

A vision is more comprehensive than a goal. A goal, which is a moment in time, specifies an objective to reach at a specific time. Vision encompasses not only where a company wants its business to go, but also what kind of company it wants to be.

This often means transforming the business. Growth requires change and a willingness to be malleable. For this particular company it meant adding new capacities to their core product which had identified them as a leader in the industry. Their strategic plan would change who they were without stripping them of their brand identity.

Initially, leadership couldn't see it because they had an operational mindset.

They gave all their energy and time to running the company. That's important, but it can be limiting. Operational thinking tends to dominate and squeeze out visionary and strategic thinking. The challenge for an established business is to shift from an operational to a strategic mindset by continually transforming the vision that gave it birth. When leadership visualizes what the company can become, they also begin to see what they can do to get there.

Structure Follows Strategy

This chapter can be summed up in two words: *Plan first*. You are undoubtedly familiar with the carpenter's proverb, "Measure twice, cut once." When applied to business, it means take the time to plan before you make a change.

I have seen it happen time and again. Entrepreneurs are idea people. However, when they chase their own ideas without following a strategic plan, they invariably get ahead of the business and make decisions which prove costly to the company. For example, owners might have an idea for a new product. Because they achieved success with their first idea, they assume subsequent ideas will also be successful.

III

Putting these wasteful operational ideas
into place is the direct result
of making the huge mistake of putting
structure before strategy.
Strategy must always lead.

IIIIIIIIIIIIIIIIIIIIIIIIIIIIIIIIIIIIIIIIIIIIIII

After expending capital—including hiring additional employees, buying new machinery, expanding facilities—to bring their product to market, they find out customers aren't buying it. Putting these wasteful operational ideas into place is a direct result of making the huge mistake of putting structure before strategy. Strategy must always lead.

The desire to pursue and implement new ideas is not the problem. Such ideas are critical to innovation and growth. The failure lies in not following a pre-established strategic plan. A good plan establishes a protocol for research and development, which includes identifying customers, their needs, and the ability to satisfy those needs. All these vital considerations are part of strategic planning.

Strategic Plan is the Map

If vision is the driver, the strategic plan is the map that gets you to where you want to be.

In a family business, the family meeting provides the impetus for a strategic plan which will facilitate a transition from one generation to the next as well as enable the company to grow.

A strategic plan is not abstract. In fact, it helps to actually visualize it by drawing a simple picture, the simpler the better. My wife and I once told an adviser we wanted to someday own a property in the Southwest, have a lake house back home in Iowa, and to volunteer with not-for-profits, among other things. Our adviser tore a corner off a napkin, drew a square, divided it into quadrants representing each goal. Today we still have that scrap of paper, and all the areas are complete, although not exactly as we had envisioned them. The picture is an ongoing reminder of how it helped us think strategically about our future after retirement.

Assess Your Mission

To get somewhere you need to start from where you are. It's a truism that many businesses simply don't follow. A strategic plan always starts with an objective assessment of the current status, using tools like a SWOT (strengths, weaknesses, opportunities, threats) analysis to help answer the question, "Where are we now?"

This assessment puts the business mission statement under scrutiny, because the mission can be defined as *"What are we doing today to help us survive?"* In most businesses, the mission gives rise to a business model which hasn't changed since the founding of the business. Companies simply pursue variations on the same business model which creates a cautious management culture, with a business- as-usual management process.

Peter Drucker argues that a company must understand its theory of business, which Drucker defines as "the assumption upon which the business was built and shapes an organization's behavior, dictates what decisions it makes, and defines the results accepted."[2]

Drucker also believes most organizations fail to keep their theories of business updated.

Reality can change quickly. You lose a customer responsible for fifty percent of your business. Your competition comes out with a new product you are not prepared to match or beat. New technology renders your product or service obsolete. All are frightening possibilities.

Companies need to be prepared to change with these shifts in their environments. To do so, they must first engage in a rigorous confrontation of reality, both external and internal. This will help them refocus. Paying attention to the shifts and making necessary adjustments to the business are critical. Companies with strategic plans will continue to prosper by identifying and developing expertise required to keep up with the changes.

How Do We Get There?

Most of the oldest generations have the uncanny ability to concentrate on the trivial facets of their businesses, when they should be focused strategically.

I've been in board meetings of multi-million-dollar companies where owners want to discuss one-hundred dollar expense items. This is a travesty. It has no place in the board room and items like this shouldn't even be considered as discussion points. It's easier, however, than thinking strategically.

Imagination is the ability of the mind to be creative or re-

2 Peter F. Drucker, "The Theory of the Business," *Harvard Business Review,* September-October, 1994.

sourceful. Transforming a company requires imagination and extensive effort, but business owners are typically too busy with daily operations to get involved in reimagining the entire business.

Asking, "Where are we now?" requires discipline and focus. Asking, "How do get to where we want to be?" requires imagination. When my colleague and I suggested to the management team the possibility of making their competitor an ally, we encouraged them to look at a hard reality and reimagine it. As a result, they turned one of their biggest obstacles into an opportunity. This required a shift in mindset from missional thinking—what's our current situation?—to visional thinking—what's our future situation?—that forms the basis of the strategic plan. When owners and management pivot from where they are now to where they want to be, and begin to think of specific ways to get there, they form the basis of a strategic plan.

Asking the right questions helps a business grasp what needs to be done. These questions revolve around the current and future value of their product or service to their clients. Can they offer new products or services to current customers? Can they offer their current products to other industries? Do they have the capacity to develop new products for new industries?

The answers to these questions help formulate action plans with specific timetables, which are assigned to various members of the management team. In this case, a strategic plan laid out the specific action steps: consider more applications for their product, acquire more workers and more plants to accommodate the growth, and train and expand the sales force to market the company's expanded services.

||||||||||||||||||||||||||||||||||||||||||||||

When owners and management
pivot from where they are now
to where they want to be,
and begin to think of specific ways
to get there, they form the basis
of a strategic plan.

||||||||||||||||||||||||||||||||||||||||||||||

All In

A strategic plan is not kept secret. I encourage owners to tell everyone in the company as soon as possible. Knowledge is power. Information motivates employees, securing their engagement, teamwork, and commitment. Employees want to know where the business is going, and what should be their focus.

The entire process of developing and executing a strategic plan must involve input from management and employees. Every member of the management team must understand the requirement to take an active role—no exceptions. Company executives need to encourage managers and employees to be brutally honest about what they see as the company's greatest weaknesses and offer ideas contributing to the transformation. When all employees are vested in the process, they are energized to contribute their ideas which accelerates the transformation. After all, they are the ones who relate directly to customers and make the company's products.

Be Brief

A strategic plan should be short. The best way to articulate a vision is to boil it down to a manageable list of no more than five or six issues, communicating only the key concepts to act upon. The best strategic plans are one to two pages. They state the most important issues, choose the team in charge of resolving each issue, and set the deadlines.

Non-stop Strategic Thinking

Once a company has formed a strategic plan, it needs to understand that the plan is continuous, not just a point in time. Family business leaders who are immersed in operations need to regularly lift the periscope to see what's ahead.

Here are ideas to make that happen:

• Designate one hour a day to think strategically, guided by the question, "Where do we want to be in five years?" Most people do not allot this time because they are driven by their TO DO lists, which typify operational thinking. They panic if they don't get them done. If they first think strategically, it is much easier to get through their TO DO lists. The most valuable takeaway from this section is that strategic thinking actually guides operational thinking. When your top and middle management take the time to think strategically as well as operationally, they help position the business for growth. Every time I hear top and middle management complain about not having the time for thinking strategically I tell them, "You can't afford to *not* make the time."

• Strategic thinking encourages the change necessary for a company to grow. This requires a change of mindset from a singular focus on operations to the kind of future thinking that brings growth. Many companies find it hard to let go of the past because they don't think out fifteen years from now. They only think about today. Developing a strategic mindset helps everyone in the company also see beyond what is directly in front of them.

• Owners of successful companies who don't have strategic plans are the hardest to convince they need one. We all know companies—even big ones—that have failed due to a lack of strategic planning. To stay off that list, keep thinking how to do things differently, which usually generates better ideas, which generate growth. Sometimes this kind of thinking is prompted by an outside perspective, such as an outside board member who asks one simple and very important question: "Why are you doing it this way?"

Even successful companies could have been more success-ful with planning. When companies don't make time to think about improving their quality, upgrading their technology, and paying attention to shifts in the market, they will struggle to stay relevant. When they don't look ahead, they'll end up be-hind everyone else.

CHAPTER 5

The Importance of an Outside Board

Business owners receive a great deal of input, feedback, and advice from customers, consultants and close associates. Unfortunately, they rarely consider one of the most important and valuable sources of advice for a family-owned or closely-held business: an outside board. Nearly eighty-five percent of these companies don't have an outside board despite the fact that companies with outside boards are healthier and last longer. However, half of the eighty-five percent don't see the need for an outside board because they believe they already have one, comprised of friends, family, or acquaintances. If you are one of those who believes that, as you read this chapter you will realize you don't have an outside board!

Outside boards are uniquely valuable because they offer independent counsel. All other sources—such as paid consultants and employees—are dependent on the business in some manner. They don't want to risk losing the benefits they receive from the business, so they tell the owner what they think the owner wants to hear.

True outside board members don't have vested interests. They are not employees, consultants, or friends of the business owner. Without these strings attached, they are free to offer independent thought motivated by a genuine desire to help the business. Outside board members are not afraid to tell business owners what they need—but often don't want—to hear. That is their primary task and responsibility. The owners need to realize board members are not there to replace them, their advisers, or their employees.

An objective and expert outside perspective is invaluable to a business, although sometimes the recommendations can be traumatic. I worked with a successful company preparing to go overseas with their product. The outside board recommended the owner hire an outside president familiar with foreign markets. "Not a chance in hell," the owner responded, and then fired the entire board. He immediately put together a new board even more qualified than the previous one.

After meeting for a year, the second board gave him the same recommendation. "This time, I knew I needed to listen," the owner told me later. After several days he began the process of hiring an outside president. Within months, the company was overseas and growing rapidly.

Three Prerequisites

There are three prerequisites for having an outside board: owners have to want an outside board, they must be willing to listen to the independent advice of the board, and they also must be willing to make changes. None of these are easy, but they are vital to the growth of the business.

Agreeing to set up an outside board acknowledges a willingness

Outside board members are not afraid to tell business owners what they need— but often don't want—to hear.

to loosen your grip on your company. Family business owners are afraid to let go because they do not understand the upside of letting go. They are not willing or able to discern the right time to let go so they continue to hang on to the detriment of the company. An outside board can help allay their fear, but only when owners realize a board looks out for the company's long-term best interests. Wanting an outside board goes hand in hand with wanting what's best for the company, which overrides the desire to be always in control.

Until owners understand this, they won't want an outside board. When they have a board, they might not want to listen, even though they know the board is telling them what they need to hear. The previously mentioned owner had to go through two boards to realize they "had his back" when they told him what he didn't want to hear. Being willing to listen was a huge realization. The upside of his letting go was the company's rapid overseas expansion.

Every business owner needs to ascribe to the Golden Rule of Listening: "Listen to others as you would have them listen to you." Listening to the board can pay huge dividends.

It's not easy to do, particularly for successful business owners who have achieved success by listening to themselves. Why listen to someone else? The desire to listen to an outside board indicates the maturing of the business owners, as well as a willingness to set their egos aside for the growth of their businesses. Few business owners arrive at this realization through self-evaluation. It comes from being repeatedly told by different people what they don't want to hear. Even if the first generation has been successful without listening to outside advice, a business can't continue to grow without it.

Building A Board

When business owners ask me, "When is the right time to assemble an outside board?" I always say, "Now!" Having a board is helpful at any point in the life cycle of any business.

Many business owners believe they need a fully-formed outside board to begin to utilize it, followed by the excuse they don't have time to look for three or four board members. I tell them to start with one person. A board takes time to build, and it doesn't need to be fully formed to be effective. Identify the greatest need in the business, then find the best person who has the expertise and experience to help in that area. The first board member can help find a second member, and the two of them a third and fourth, if needed, until the board is complete. I recommend no more than seven board members, with the family in the majority. More than seven, the board becomes cumbersome. Fewer than seven will not provide enough diversity of independent thought.

Who's on Board

The makeup of an effective outside board is largely dependent on *what the business needs, not who the owner knows.* When owners stock the board with choice picks—someone they know, or a big name in the industry or the community—the focus shifts from the importance of what the business needs to who's on the board. A business cannot afford for this to happen. It cannot include friends, acquaintances, or anyone who is dependent on the owners, or has ties to the company. As I have noted, such members cannot offer independent thought, and business sessions can easily become merely social events.

Business needs should drive the selection of board members. It is usually a good idea for owners to choose a majority of new board members from companies larger than their own. If you are considering a transition plan, find another business owner who has been through a successful transition. If you need marketing and branding help, you could look for someone in a public company who would be willing to serve on the board. Personnel from public companies are well-trained experts in the field who can offer the needed experience and perspective. Coming from outside your industry, they will not be constricted by conventional industry thinking. Their vantage point will prompt them to ask tough questions insiders would not think to ask. Questions like: "Why are you doing this?" or "Why are you doing it this way? or "Based on my experience, I've never heard of doing it this way." Such questions invite owners to rethink their business processes.

When board members are being considered, I often hear two complementary questions: one from the owners, "Why would *they* want to be on my board?" and one from the prospective board members, "Why do they want *me* on their board?" These questions indicate the right people are under consideration.

Many potential board members don't see themselves as having anything to offer. I believe owners who are running or have run successful businesses can be great assets on a board, if they don't wait too long after they have retired. The potential of serving on an outside board can provide the final impetus for aging business owners to let go of their own businesses and make a significant contribution to someone else's business. They can still be in the game, still have significance, and, most importantly, contribute their wealth of knowledge and experience to someone who needs it.

Equip Your Board

Once the right people are on the board, business owners need to equip them with the right tools to do the job. Otherwise, their expertise is wasted.

To ensure this doesn't happen, owners should withhold nothing from board members. They need to see everything to provide an accurate diagnosis, and give correct advice based on reality, not an airbrushed picture of the business. This includes a tour of the facility, access to all financials two weeks prior to a board meeting, and comprehensive reports from upper management. The president's direct reports should present regularly to the board, answer questions from the board members, and then leave the meeting. This helps the board members look at the company from the different perspectives of the leadership team, who might address issues the owner is unaware of or is hesitant to discuss. If management reports regularly, the board gets to know the team, their strengths and weaknesses, and can make personnel recommendations to the owner.

Paying Your Board

Outside board members should never ask, "How much do I get paid?" Money cannot be the motivator. They should do it because they want to help. Having achieved business success themselves, these leaders appreciate the opportunity to share their knowledge to help others succeed.

However, money must be a part of the contract. Board members need to be paid for their services. Money acknowledges both their expertise and their value to the company. As a rule of thumb, I recommend owners calculate what they take out of the company every year, divided by two thousand hours. Pay board members that rate for every hour the board meets and also cover their expenses. The payment is more symbolic than it is monetary, as it doesn't reflect the true worth board members bring to the company.

The value an outside board brings to a company will far exceed what the members are paid. When you pay the board members the same hourly rate as the owner it indicates they are as important as the owner. Also important is the value of their time. Every year a calendar for the next year's board meetings should be agreed upon. If any board members cannot attend a pre-determined board meeting they should still be paid. This will also assure the board members they are valued by the owners.

Term Limits for Board Members

Board members should serve long enough to have become familiar with the company, and effectively apply their knowledge, but not to the extent that they have exhausted all their knowledge. This generally means four to five two-year terms, with performance evaluations each term. Every board member should evaluate every other person on the board. Evaluations can either be seen by everyone on the board, or, I recommend they be reviewed by the owner, who then determines whether or not to

||||||||||||||||||||||||||||||||||||||||||||

An outside board often becomes a business owner's invaluable asset and ally.

||||||||||||||||||||||||||||||||||||||||||||

keep the board member. As with advisers and the management team, board members need to be dismissed when the company outgrows them. Thank outgoing members for their help to the company and tell them you simply need someone with a different type of expertise suited to the company's current and future needs. Be sure to stagger the terms so there isn't more than one member leaving at the same time.

Everything to Gain

There is no downside to having an outside board. There is everything to gain, and everyone gains—business owners, board members, employees, as well as the business itself. Some owners fear losing control if they hire an outside board. This is a false fear. The business owner is always in control and can fire the board at any time, as did the owner who did not like the idea he should bring in a new president. He was in control when he hired a new board and still in control when he finally let go and brought in a president.

Owners can trust board members because their intention is to help the business, not themselves. They want to see the business grow and thrive. An outside board often becomes a business owner's invaluable asset and ally.

CHAPTER 6

The Value of Good Advice

The older gentleman in the back of the room raised his hand, and I knew what was coming.

"I don't agree with any of this bulls__ you're spewing!"

My business associate and I had been talking with the management team about the future of the company and the changes they needed to make. These were not my ideas. The so-called "spewing" was actually me reporting what the management team told us during our strategic planning process. The discussion had turned to the opportunities for the company to expand into new areas.

"You don't even want to think about what else your company could be doing?" I asked.

"We've never done that before," he responded, "and I'm not going to put up with this." With that, he walked out of the room.

The following week, the owners walked him out of the company, along with a severance package. It was time for him to go, and for the company to let him go, even though he had been with them since his early twenties.

His natural instinct was to protect the company's success, and be risk averse because the business had too much to lose. He thought he was being loyal, but his loyalty was to the company as it had been, not what it needed to become. It's also why I immediately reported his actions to the owners. The company couldn't afford to have a manager whose reaction was, "Why change?" These are the "hangers-on" in a company. They hang on too long to what they know, and won't let go.

One of the laws of change is, as soon as you try something new, you'll get resistance.

"We have never done that before" is a statement of resistance. It will strangle a business if allowed any air time. If you hear it, you need to banish it from the company, sometimes along with the people who say it. This statement of resistance may sound innocent, but it indicates overconfidence in your current business model, even if it is outdated, and it shuts the door on new thinking.

A changing of the old guard is not easy, especially if they have loyally served the company since day one. This is when practical consequences must override deep-seated emotional attachment and affection for these employees.

It's Not Going to Happen to Me

The flip side of overconfidence is denial. About fifty percent of marriages end in divorce, but around the time of the wedding ceremony almost all couples believe there is approximately zero percent chance it will happen to them. A similar point applies to entrepreneurs starting new businesses, where the failure rate is greater than fifty percent. In one survey respondents were asked to rate their chance of success. Many answered, "One-hundred percent." Just as most people underestimate the likelihood they will be divorced or in a car accident or suffer major diseases, the prevailing thought is, "It's not going to happen to me."

I have previously noted the fear of dying, in a contradictory way, feeds into a sense of unrealistic optimism. No one likes to think about dying and this mindset transfers to everything they do, especially when things are going well: "If we keep doing what we've always done, things will go as they've always gone. Why change a good thing?"

This is another mindset causing a failure to plan for the future of the business. When business owners overestimate their immunity from harm, they fail to take sensible preventive steps. Failing to put a transition plan in place and refusing to change the way it's always been done are crucial mistakes.

Start Now

Old is not just about aging. It's also a mindset, a hardening of the categories—the perception is old ways are not just the best ways, they are the only way. A business can become irrelevant very quickly if it doesn't start out with a plan for enabling growth through continual change and innovation. In the early days of a business you make choices—consciously and unconsciously—which will influence your culture far into the future. Those choices will become patterns, either limiting or enhancing your ability to thrive and transition to succeeding generations.

It's never too early—or too late—to build change into the organizational operating system of your company. Create room to grow by being open to new ideas inviting change. The important thing is to start doing it now.

The S-Curve

A critical turning point occurs when a business needs to innovate and find a way to stay relevant, so it can continue to grow. All businesses have their own S-curves, which is well documented in financial writings. Noted here is the basic trajectory from start-up (survival mode), to growth, to a tapering off point. Prior to the tapering off point, when a business transitions to the next generation a new S-curve is created. Good advisers help business owners navigate the S-curves.

THE S-CURVE OF A BUSINESS

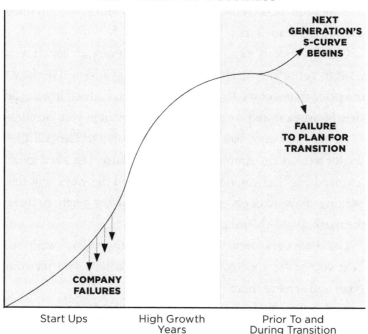

NEXT
GENERATION'S
S-CURVE
BEGINS

FAILURE
TO PLAN FOR
TRANSITION

COMPANY
FAILURES

Start Ups   High Growth   Prior To and
             Years   During Transition

Hiring good advisers is a challenge for family and closely-held businesses. Most don't have sufficient capital to hire the best advisers, especially when they are starting out at the very beginning of the S-curve, because they feel the need to pour all available money into operational costs. What they don't understand in the early stages is how vital it is to get good advice. It is critical to the long-term success of the business, even though it may be more expensive. During my more than forty years of experience with many family-owned businesses, choosing whether or not to hire good advisers was at the top or near the top of the list of major decisions they made.

Invest in Advice

It can't be stressed enough: a business must seek good advice to achieve success. What a business needs more than anything else are good advisers.

Good advice is expensive but worth every dollar. If you want to get by on the cheap, you get cheap advice. This is not the place to cut costs. Pay the price for good advice from experienced advisers and consider it an investment in your business.

Henry Ford once balked at paying $10,000 to General Electric for work done troubleshooting a generator. He asked for an itemized bill. The engineer who performed the work sent this: "Making chalk mark on generator, $1. Knowing where to make the mark, $9,999." Ford paid the bill.

Good advisers know where to "make the mark," where to help you make your mark, and where to help you set your goals and achieve them.

As I have noted, the dilemma is smaller businesses need good advice the most but are least able to afford it. Knowing this, good advisers are understandably reluctant to help smaller businesses.

This is when small business owners need to consider the value of sacrifice.

A Sacrificial Investment

The essence of sacrifice is giving up something of value now for something better in the future. Businesses that eventually thrive know the importance of making short-term sacrifices which will yield long-term gain. It's why successful business owners work sixteen hours a day for themselves. Understanding the value of sacrifice, delayed gratification, and bargaining with the future make it possible to find a way to invest in the best advisers.

Prioritizing the role of advisers in your business is not only an investment of money and resources, it's also an investment of time. Take the time to get it right. I can't stress this enough. It never pays to rush this critical stage of setting up your business. With the aid of technology, it is easier than ever to start a business, and accomplish it with less capital than it used to require. In these circumstances it is also much easier to rush into it. Do your research. Think through your core product and your core customers. Start with one product, get it right, for the right customers. The opportunities for growth and expansion will always be there, but only if you get it right in the beginning stages. Remember, money runs out faster than opportunities.

Listening to Your Advisers

Advice is only as good as your ability to listen to it. This does not include listening to yourself and following your own advice.

||||||||||||||||||||||||||||||||||||||||||||||

Remember, money runs out faster
than opportunities.

||||||||||||||||||||||||||||||||||||||||||||||

It's impossible to be your own adviser. Self-talk doesn't generate new ideas. It recycles old ideas, making you think you have new ideas. Meaningful and significant change comes from listening to someone who has already been where you are today or has the experience of working with other companies in your situation. As I have noted, the time will come when you have to stop listening to old advisers because your company has outgrown them. Wise owners will acknowledge this and bring in new blood.

The Right Question

You won't get good answers unless your advisers have good questions. The best advisers know to ask the right questions to get the information they need. The question I have found most helpful is, "Why are you doing that?" It's both focused and open, and gets the conversation happening fast and deep. Advisers learn what they need to know about your business, and why you're doing what you do. This helps you and your advisers explore the possibilities of doing something differently.

A Second Opinion

The older gentleman, mentioned earlier, who walked out on me, had been a member of a trusted management team for decades, until his advice was no longer reliable. Just as a patient benefits from a second medical opinion, a business owner needs to hear from multiple advisers and multiple generations. The likelihood you are getting good advice increases the more times you hear the same advice from different people.

As your company matures it is imperative to transition your team of advisers, as well as your top managers, selecting a team which also represents the next generation. The generation taking over will resent advisers who have been with the company from the beginning and who tell them their parents and grandparents "never did it that way."

Run It by the Board

Advisers are paid and they often have an area of specialty. Both may limit their objectivity. As I have noted, anyone on the company payroll is dependent on the business in some manner. Paid advisers may have an inherent bias toward telling owners what they want to hear. If advisers are hired for their expertise in a certain area, they don't always have the big picture in mind. I recommend you run any advice from your advisers by the outside board, which does not have the same conflict of interests.

This recommendation is an effective use of both your advisers and your board. Advisers inject innovative ideas and suggestions into the board's discussions, which the board can then decide whether or not to incorporate into their advice for the business.

A Company of Advisers

Your management team and employees can be a source of good advice.

Managers will give you better advice if they are attentive to

||||||||||||||||||||||||||||||||||||||||||||||

I encourage you to assemble your most trusted advisers and say, "I died last night. What happens next"?

||||||||||||||||||||||||||||||||||||||||||||||

your employees. In healthy companies, communication flows not only from the top down but also from the bottom up. Ideas are gathered and channeled from the managers to the executive team. When a company implements any of these ideas, employees know they are being heard and respected.

When managers listen, employees will become, in effect, a company of advisers. Managers who learn to ask employees questions, instead of telling them what to do, will find they often have invaluable insights to offer the company. The employees will feel they have significance beyond simply doing their jobs. Knowing they have real input into the company's direction and purpose, employees will not only take pride in their work, they will feel what they do contributes to the success of their company.

I Died Last Night

I know several owners of companies who used a startling method of checking preparedness of their outside advisers and management teams. Each of the owners individually gathered these important people into their boardrooms for a surprise meeting.

When all were present the owner said, "I died last night. Now tell me what's going to happen?" The question typically stumps the advisers, who usually end up disagreeing over the outcome because they had never considered how the owner's sudden death might impact every area of the business. Ultimately, they had not prepared the company for this critical situation.

I want to stress that advisers must think about death of owners at all ages. Death has no regard for age, yet younger owners almost never think of it happening to them. If given the opportunity, I wake them up to the reality of death or incapacity. When a company has more than one owner, I often ask them, "Where does the stock go if one of you dies or becomes incapacitated?"

"To one of the spouses," is the usual answer.

"Do you want that spouse to be your partner?" I ask.

Their reaction is usually, "Definitely not!"

Thinking about death can clarify our lives. It helps us know how we want to live. It also helps us understand how much we want what we've built to continue after we're gone.

It's not enough to plan only for the transition of your company. Your advisers need to plan for your death, extending your life's work into the following generations. Not planning for your death will not only be traumatic for your family, but also for your business.

I encourage you to assemble your most trusted advisers and say, "I died last night. What happens next?"

CHAPTER 7

Letting Go

The statement was understandable, coming from someone who had never started and owned a business.

"Why won't my father-in-law let go of the company?"
I was at dinner in Mexico with a family business owner's
daughter and her husband. Both worked for the company. I
responded to him with a question: "How old is your youngest
child?"

"About one year old."

"I have a deal for you," I said. "Why don't you give him to
me, and I'll raise him for the next five years?"

"Why would I want to do that?"

"Why wouldn't you?" I replied. "I promise I'll take good care
of him, see to his education, and treat him like he's one of ours."

"There's no way in hell!" he said, looking confused and
upset at this turn in the conversation.

"Okay, now, let's talk about why your father-in-law doesn't
want to give up his company," I said. At that instance I noticed
his wife nodding her head in agreement, immediately getting
my point.

I've had variations of this conversation with many clients over the 40-plus years I've worked with family-owned businesses. The notion of equating a parent's child with that of how founders feel about their businesses is an analogy that holds true.

Letting go is probably one of the hardest things—if not the hardest thing—an owner will ever have to do.

My Company, My Identity

Business owners devote their lives to starting, building and growing their businesses. They've risked everything for the survival of their companies. It's their baby. Their lifeblood. Their identity. As one business owner said to me when he was feeling pressured to call it quits: "That's my damn name on that building, and I'll stay here as long as I want."

I once worked with a company owned by two aging brothers with opposing views of letting go. The younger one said, "I'm done. Let the sons take over. I don't have an issue. I have a lot of things outside of work—with our church, the school, and not-for-profits."

I asked, "What does your older brother do outside of the company?"

"Nothing. If he retires, he's going to die in his chair."

Many business owners don't retire because they don't know what they'll do that will provide as much meaning as running their companies. They fear irrelevance, afraid no one will pick up the phone to discuss business issues or ask for their advice. No one wants to feel unimportant and unneeded.

Many, though, simply have nothing to retire to. *What am I gonna do? Just sit home all day?*

Many business owners are focused only on their companies

⸻

Letting go is probably one of the hardest things—if not the hardest thing— an owner will ever have to do.

⸻

and haven't developed interests or relationships outside of their work world. The solution offered by numerous advisers and family members is the owner should pick up a hobby or travel the world! This type of advice shows that neither the advisers nor the family members have any empathy for what the owner is going through. Frankly, it's more difficult to develop hobbies later in life, making it even harder to let go.

My approach to this topic with owners is a bit different. I like to help business owners reframe the idea of letting go as an opportunity to actually gain something. It's much easier to let go when you have other interests. I tell them not to retire *from* the business, but to retire *to* something. While it can take time to figure out exactly what that something is, owners can find meaning and make valuable contributions outside the business.

I also talk about their age, and reason with them: "At this point in time, you have enough wealth to live on for the rest of your life, so why don't you try to enjoy it? I know you thrive on running the company, but why don't you share your knowledge?" Not-for-profit organizations, for instance, need business leaders on their boards. I've even worked with some business owners who have launched their own nonprofits in their retirement years. Also, retired business owners can pour their acumen and passion into smaller companies, which often need investors as well as board members.

The conversation typically goes something like this:

"Why would a company want me on their board?"

"You've run a successful company," I reply. "And people like you are valued for your wisdom. You have much to offer, or your company would not have been successful. Other business owners love receiving ideas from successful people."

Hearing these options while considering retirement often lifts the owner's self-esteem. Retirement is not an end but a transition, which often begins years in advance with the question: "What can I retire to?" Business owners need to think about how they are going to transition themselves, not just their companies.

The family business needs its founder to let go. The family also needs the founder to be a parent and a grandparent who finds fulfillment in something other than the business. In this way, the transition ensures not only the business survives but also that the family thrives into the next generation.

Having worked with a business owner for five years, I kept recommending she retire and become Chairman of the Board. For years she was reluctant to give up her day-to-day involvement in the company. But she did. A few months after making the transition, she called me, saying, "Well, we finally took your advice and did what you recommended. Everything's better. The company is doing better, and I'm much happier."

If business owners are going to give up the very thing that has defined them, it is essential to look for opportunities which

⁞⁞⁞⁞⁞⁞⁞⁞⁞⁞⁞⁞⁞⁞⁞⁞⁞⁞⁞⁞⁞⁞⁞⁞⁞⁞⁞⁞⁞⁞⁞⁞⁞⁞

I tell them not to retire <u>from</u> the business but to retire <u>to</u> something.

⁞⁞⁞⁞⁞⁞⁞⁞⁞⁞⁞⁞⁞⁞⁞⁞⁞⁞⁞⁞⁞⁞⁞⁞⁞⁞⁞⁞⁞⁞⁞⁞⁞⁞

exist outside of their companies. When owners try something different, they often find they enjoy not having to live with the day-to-day pressures of running a company.

Getting Out of the Way

While letting go is incredibly difficult for those who can't picture life in retirement, often there's another reason for not retiring. It's hard to let the next generation take over. I worked with two brothers who co-owned a company, and they couldn't get along, even with offices side by side. Employees overheard screaming matches between the two.

For years, we tried to figure out a way to transition the business to the next generation. It always came to a dead-end: one brother's son worked in the company, and the other brother didn't think his nephew was capable of leading the company. His solution was to stay in leadership, so the promotion of his nephew never happened. Months passed, and one day I called up another of their advisers, who had also been unable to help them, saying, "The problem has been resolved."

"You've got to be kidding me!" the adviser said. "What happened?"

"One brother died."

This is an outcome I hope to never face again.

In this case, the delay prevented the new leader from taking the reins of the business. Entering into a long-term decline, the company needed the nephew's energy and fresh ideas long before the death of his uncle.

Often sons or daughters yearn for a chance to prove themselves. They are eager for an opportunity to run the company. However, an owner who risked everything to build the business often balks at any notion of "It's time for you to step aside." If they've paved the way, it's hard for them to step out of the way. The tendency for owners is to hang on even tighter, thus preventing the next generation from ever stepping into leadership roles. Sometimes owners work so long—well into their eighties— their potential family successors are near retirement.

In that sense, they rob the next generation of the chance to lead the company.

Some owners don't relinquish their hold because they flat out don't trust the next generation. Believing they are not educated or experienced enough, they wonder, "How could anybody else understand the business the way we do and do as good a job running it as we did?"

While discussing this apparent roadblock, I ask the same question time and time again: "How old were you when you took over this company?"

"I was twenty-four."

"You don't think your forty-year-old daughter has enough experience in this company to run it?"

"It doesn't seem like she does."

The great irony is, it was okay for the owner to start working in the company at age twenty-four, but it's not all right for daughters or sons to provide leadership at age forty. As a general rule, the younger generation tends to be more mentally agile. They are certainly more technologically savvy, and are often willing to take the risk to grow the business that a business owner is done taking. They often can see the decline of the family business more clearly, and have the risk-taking energy to set it back on track.

Same Old Thing, Same Old Result

Lack of risk-taking goes hand-in-hand with stale thinking. I've had conversations with frustrated management teams of aging owners sharing their thoughts: "They don't bring as much value to the company anymore. They control the meetings. We argue. And then we go back to doing the same thing we did before."

Of course, the same old way gets the same old results—which is why the company is in decline. Worse, rarely does someone talk directly to the owner about the issues. On the occasion they do, well-intended conversations often end in arguments. It seems easier in the short term to stay silent, though everyone is discussing it among themselves and worrying about the future of the company.

Without a transition plan in place, employees, customers, and suppliers begin to question: "How long will this company be around? What happens if the owner dies and there isn't a transition plan? Will the company and our jobs even survive?" Employees worried about job security will look for work elsewhere. Customers and suppliers begin shoring up more secure relationships. More critically, most of these questions and concerns are not heard or understood by the owners.

All this anxiety can help accelerate the company's decline.

ll

The most important step in letting go
is the first: to imagine both the necessity
of the transition process
and the willingness to let go.

llllllllllllllllllllllllllllllllllllllll

Ironically, the owner hangs on tighter the more the company declines.

As helpful as it might be, a magical "let it go" age doesn't exist. Every company is different. Every family is different. There are seventy-year-old leaders who run companies very well, and there are fifty-eight-year-olds who don't. Age isn't the only decider. The current and future health of the company should be a major discussion in the decision-making process.

To bridge the gap from doing everything to taking on a different role, I often recommend business owners move up to the position of Chairman of the Board. That typically includes moving their offices outside of the building. This allows them to remain part of the company—they attend board meetings while providing input and casting their vision for the company—without interfering with the day-to-day leadership.

Moving the owner's office to another location is vital. Having the next president occupy the vacated office of the owner will have two very important effects. First, it will immediately show the direct reports that the owner is no longer easily accessible to them. They will quickly learn they need to go to the new president. Secondly, this move will show the employees the transition is a reality.

It is important to mention that some business owners hang on too long because they perceive they haven't socked away enough for retirement. Though a rarity, some haven't. One option is to sell the company to the next generation at a thirty to forty percent discount. That serves a dual purpose. The sale provides liquidity for the owner's retirement while ensuring the next generation has some "skin in the game." Companies given to the next generation have a tendency not to fare as well as those acquired by the next generation. Investing in the company is critical, as it makes the next generation responsible for their actions.

Making decisions related to letting go are all part of the transition plan. As we have seen, transitions happen over a period of time and are comprised of a number of steps. Each step must be taken to complete the transition. Similarly, letting go isn't a moment in time either. It's also a process comprised of steps.

The most important step in letting go is the first: to imagine both the necessity of the transition process and the willingness to let go.

CHAPTER 8

Passion— You Can't Lead Without It

started the family meeting with a very sensitive statement to all the family members, each of whom I had previously interviewed.

"I have one thing to tell you," I began. "Outside of your parents, not one of you has a passion for this company. Without that passion, it's unlikely this company will survive."

Two siblings shot back in unison, "We do too have passion!"

"No, you don't and here's why. When you arrive late to work, leave early, and go to lunch together, you know what you're telling your employees? That you don't care. That's it's up to them to carry this company."

They were silent.

"You carry it. Show them how you love this company. One more thing. Leave the luxury cars at home!"

I called this family out on the one thing a company must

〰〰〰〰〰〰〰〰〰〰〰

A family business simply can't afford to carry family members who don't have passion for the company.

〰〰〰〰〰〰〰〰〰〰〰

have: passionate leadership. None of the next generation had passion for the company, because it hadn't been demanded of them. Their parents had stoked the fire for years, and the children were simply basking in its warmth. At some point the next generation has to start feeding that fire because passion is the heart of a thriving family business.

For a successful transition, a family business must find a way to transmit passion to the next generation. Without passion they will struggle to lead. The succeeding generation should have developed passion for the company prior to the transition by learning all facets of the business, and by becoming acquainted with as many employees as possible. It might take a few starts and stops and redirects for the next generation to tap into what they truly love to do, when they can say, "This is it!"

I experienced those starts and stops. My high school counselor advised me to major in engineering because I excelled in math. I quickly discovered I wasn't good at engineering so I left college and was a hired hand on a farm for a year while I was still searching. Accounting was my next choice for a career path although I didn't expect my first accounting job would be doing government accounting while in the Air Force. After serving four years I then finished college and was hired by Arthur Andersen & Co. where I was introduced to the world of family-owned and closely-held businesses. That's when I knew "this is it!"

When I advise family members I help them determine if "this is it," which is demonstrated by their commitment to work. They can't remain in idle. They have to go full throttle or get out. If they're not passionate, I encourage them to leave and do something else. A family business simply can't afford to carry family members who don't have passion for the company.

Employees, customers and vendors can detect when passion is no longer the rudder of an organization. Lack of passion in leadership creates organizational apathy and calls into question the credibility and direction of the business. Passion is essential for leadership of any kind, but especially for building a business which demands the highest level of dedication and persistence. It's not up to employees to carry the weight of the business on their shoulders. The family leaders need to carry it and show employees they're in it with them.

All the Talent in the World

I describe passion as the active ingredient in a chemical reaction. Many of the ingredients necessary for a chemical reaction are inactive, but when they are combined with the one active ingredient in the right circumstances, things happen. Passion is that active ingredient.

An athlete can have tremendous talent and innate ability, but without passionate drive and grit that athlete will not succeed. The same is true in business. Talent and skill, whether it be in technology, engineering, finance, or other areas, cannot make up for a lack of passion. In fact, all the talent in the world is

||||||||||||||||||||||||||||||||||||||||||||

*I describe passion as the active ingredient
in a chemical reaction.*

||||||||||||||||||||||||||||||||||||||||||||

meaningless without it.

Meaningful and productive talent must be activated and coordinated by passionate leadership. Passion energizes leadership. In turn, passionate leaders ignite passion in their employees. It is contagious. When the employees catch it the company can soar.

Pick the Passionate One

When family business owners pick their successors, they often default to the one most talented or charismatic. But talent or charisma do not necessarily translate into passion. Neither do the other traditional markers by which owners tend to choose, such as age, gender, or seniority.

After one family meeting I told the parents, "Your daughter needs to be your next leader." Surprised, they asked me, "Why not our son?" "He's such a nice boy," the mother added.

"He's in sales," I said, "and good at it. However, he is totally focused on sales and does not understand the other parts of the company. It's all about him and beating his sales numbers. He can't see past his sales to consider the bigger picture—the employees, the team building, and developing the leadership skills necessary to carry your business forward."

"But sales are what make our company grow."

"Then let him keep selling," I told them, "but make your daughter the president. She's the one with the passion for the company."

Their daughter developed her passion in part by spending time with her father. She wanted to learn about every aspect of the business. For this, she had to be constantly at her father's side, do what her father did, absorb his values, his sense of purpose, and his moral compass. Also, by observing her older brother verbally mistreat employees in front of others, the daughter learned to take them aside, listen to them, and work out solutions together.

It's easy to mistake qualities such as charisma or talent for the best leadership values, including listening, delegating, and supporting employees' initiatives. When filling their top positions, closely-held companies should prioritize these values. What makes candidates good in particular areas tends to disqualify them from leadership simply because their focus and priorities are too narrow. In reality, leaders can emerge from many different positions in the company. Instead of building their own egos, these passionate leaders build the businesses they run and develop the people they lead.

Show Me Your Passion

I return to the definition of an entrepreneur from a previous chapter. Entrepreneurs are willing to work sixteen hours a day instead of working eight hours a day for someone else.

You might ask why would people work that hard? It's because they are doing what they love.

When I encourage people to do what they love, I focus as much on the loving as the doing. Passion creates a synergy. As you harness skills, talents, and aptitude to do the work, your love for it will grow. The proof of the passion is in the work ethic, as well as in producing the product or providing a service.

Passion does not necessarily follow a conventional path. For instance, if a person wants to be a welder and wants to go to welding school instead of college, I advise that person, "Do it! Go be a welder. Maybe you'll end up welding the best sculpture or most magnificent bridge this city has ever seen!"

It's not just doing what you love that ignites passion. It's also having the motivation to do what the situation calls you to do. This is certainly true for building and leading a business where duties and demands sometimes call for more than eight-hour work days. Passion keeps a leader working well beyond "business hours." Work ethic is more than just working hard. It's working with a sense of purpose and responsibility that only happens when work is more than a job.

This describes entrepreneurs. Passion fuels their work, and that passion becomes evident, not just in what they are doing but how they are doing it.

When I meet with a family, I ask the president or a family member to give me a tour of their operation. I want to see their passion in action. I am also watching particularly for two things: how they interreact with employees and how engaged they are with their product. For instance, do they take delight in making their product?

On one of these tours I watched an owner call everyone in the shop by name, and stop to ask an employee to "tell Les a little bit about what we do." Ten minutes later the employee was still telling us, and the owner didn't stop him until he was finished. These are employees who have "caught" the owner's passion because they know how much they are valued. They are proud to work there, and proud of what they do. That same owner turned around and went even deeper into explaining their product, showing me how tiny robots test tolerances to one millionth of an inch. When one millionth of an inch matters, that's passion!

The Accountability of Passion

When crafting machinery, tolerances are critical. That statement applies to people as well as machines.

People with passion hold themselves to a high standard of quality and excellence, a discipline which they consistently maintain. If they are out of tolerance they make corrections, as they do with the equipment they produce. They are not afraid of objective performance evaluations which help them stay on track and achieve their business goals. Good business owners apply these objective measures to themselves first, and then to their employees.

Administered with care, objective performance evaluations are helpful for employees. However, I have found numerous family businesses use subjective evaluations, which are neither fair nor helpful to the employees. To promote employees because they are likable or demote them because they lack people skills undermines morale and is most likely inconsistent with a company's values. It communicates to the entire work force that evaluations don't matter.

These evaluations also do for employees what a P&L does for the company. They put a number on it. They measure progress against attainable goals. It's vital that supervisors and employees work together to establish these goals, making employees responsible for their own development. The evaluation is an agreement, not a mandate. If employees don't achieve the expected results, encourage them to make corrections, develop skills, and manage resources and time, which will help them achieve the agreed-upon results. Also, expectations can be adjusted. It's as valuable to know what you can't do as to know what you can. In some cases, employees discover they are in the wrong jobs. An objective performance evaluation can redirect them toward work for which they are better suited. This may be inside or outside the company.

The Rest of the Story

"Les, you wouldn't believe how he's taken the reins."

The owner was right. I couldn't believe it. This was the company with family members I had confronted for having no passion. The father's oldest son has now stepped up. "How did that happen?" I asked.

"I didn't think he'd get it. The company had been repeatedly on the verge of bankruptcy, and I kept bailing it out. Last time this happened I pulled the family together and said, 'That's it. I'm not putting another cent into this company. I have enough to live on. All of you can find other jobs.'"

"Well, that did it, Les."

I had given the advice, but the father brought it home to the children. One of them finally woke up to his passion.

CHAPTER 9

The Entitlement Trap

A family business owner gifted a large amount of stock to the children, resulting in what was thought to be an efficient estate planning tool. Instead, it would eventually tear the family apart.

The owner meant well, but had fallen into one of the most common and debilitating parent traps of family businesses: giving shares to all the children, whether or not they work in the business.

Shares widely held among all family members is a common practice laden with good intentions, but owners don't anticipate the problems it most certainly creates. That's because the practice arises from the deeply-rooted problem of raising children to believe they are entitled, so it follows that the owner automatically gives equal shares to each child. Accountants and attorneys are also a big part of the problem. They recommend equal shares be given to the children as part of their tax planning without any thought of the long-term consequences on the family and the business.

Entitlement permeates all aspects of family dynamics, but in the family business arena I define it very specifically: Entitlement is when the children of the next generation feel it's their right to have ownership in the company, whether or not they work in the company.

A Culture of Entitlement

Entitlement is one of the most destructive forces in a family business. It is difficult to prevent, and once it's part of the family culture, it's even more difficult to eliminate. Some describe entitlement as "the kiss of death," an apt metaphor which speaks to the challenge of maintaining healthy family relationships without being indulgent. Entitlement is like a weed growing along with the good seed, inhibiting its growth. Parents are often not aware they are creating an environment where entitlement mentality can grow and gain hold. This compounds the problem.

Entitlement crops up for many reasons. Perhaps the older generations feel guilty about pouring more energy into the business than into their children's lives, so they give them the family business. Or, perhaps the children have never learned the value of hard work, but believe it's their right to own the business.

The cases of parents' bribing their children's way into college is an extreme example, but it effectively illustrates the dangers of an entitlement mentality in a family. Advancement is not based on accomplishment, but on wealth, status, and privilege. When parents give their children what they haven't earned, they prevent those children from learning a sense of

||||||||||||||||||||||||||||||||||||||||||

Entitlement is when the children of the next generation feel it's their right to have ownership in the company, whether or not they work in the company.

||||||||||||||||||||||||||||||||||||||||||

responsibility and accomplishment, forming their identities, confronting adversity, working within limits, and developing resilience. Without learning these lessons, entitlement inhibits children from growing up and makes them feel their parents don't believe in them.

I have previously mentioned the children who worked in the family business but were cavalier in their attitude. Yet, they continued to receive significant salary increases each year. They never had to earn their positions, which were given to them. This fostered a "Why not me?" mentality that undermined the work ethic and values which built the business.

The Trap of Widely-Owned Shares

In a family business, entitlement manifests itself in the way parents give ownership in the company to their children. They base it on relationship rather than merit. It's a form of nepotism, whether it's a management position in the company for which the child is not qualified, or shares they haven't worked to own. Parents believe they are treating their children equally by giving shares to all of them, whether or not they work in the company. This is naïve thinking.

First, parents don't realize their attempt at being equal is actually unfair to the children who work for the company, and carry the disproportionate burden and risk of running it. Secondly, parents don't realize this will exacerbate natural sibling rivalry, leading to conflict between the siblings who work in the company and those who don't. Ultimately, it is another entitlement trap.

I spoke with a family member whose sister worked in the family business for a number of years, helping the company prosper. This experience made her the obvious sibling to acquire the shares and run the company. Her brother saw it differently, as he looked at it through his entitled eyes and believed he had as much right to acquire shares as she did.

"She has it made," he said. "She's going to own the company."

"What if the company goes under?" I asked.

"That won't happen," he said. This is a very common belief of children from family businesses. They don't believe their family business would ever fail.

"But if it does, will you help her out?"

His response was emphatic. "Not a chance. That's her problem, and her failure."

This typifies the attitude outsiders have toward insiders. They assume the family business is the goose that continues to lay golden eggs, and never consider how fragile a business is. Often family members on the outside want the golden egg but don't want to care for the goose.

Conflict will usually arise as it separates outsiders from insiders. The outside siblings feel left out of the inner workings of the company, which they believe they are entitled to know; the inside siblings often fail to communicate how the business is progressing. The outsiders don't have any skin in the game, but want to run on the field disrupting play. They mistake their feeling of entitlement with the actual authority to have any say in how the business is managed. It's an authority they don't have.

For instance, outside shareholders do not have the right to walk into the family business and talk to employees unless they have received permission to do so. The entitlement trap can become especially disruptive if family members are on the Board of Directors. They often feel being on the board gives them additional rights to have access to the company. Outside shareholders only have two rights: the right to see the financial statements, and the right to vote, if they have voting stock. When these outside shareholders, who are family members, presume they are entitled to additional rights, they will begin to put tremendous pressure on the insiders who are running the company.

They also believe they are entitled to more of the company's wealth. This can be especially problematic when the outside shareholders perceive their inside siblings are withholding that wealth from them. As the adage goes, a little knowledge is a dangerous thing, especially when we make assumptions from what little we know. When outside shareholders are not receiving dividends while the siblings inside the company are perceived to be doing very well, they begin to question. Without satisfactory communication from the inside, questions will lead to disputes. The conflict will continue until it tears a company apart and causes its sale or its failure to survive.

Shares gifted to family members outside the company automatically entitle them to feel they can help call the shots, which undermines leadership. When it comes to company shares gifted to family, I advocate drawing a hard line between family members who work in the business and those who don't. This firewall protects the business from family or generational rivalry. If the outsiders already own shares, buy them back at a fair price. This fair buy-back price will give the outsiders the financial opportunity to follow their own passions instead of meddling in the family business.

When Entitlement Gets in the Way of Work

A father told his daughter that he was very upset with her as she always came to work late. Her response to him was, "If you weren't my father, I would come in fifteen minutes early." After that conversation, she was never late again.

When a sense of entitlement becomes a part of the family business culture, it affects every aspect of the company. It's a cancer that saps the vitality of a business and compromises the integrity of its work. This is especially true if family members work in the family business when they don't have the qualifications, experience, or passion.

That's another entitlement trap because parents assume their children want to work in the business, when they might want to pursue a different career instead. It not only hurts the business but also the children. Parents who hand their children jobs they haven't earned are telling them they can't achieve something on their own. Entitlement forces family members into a twilight zone of underperformance and discontent.

The best way for parents to help children succeed is to treat them as individuals, not as reflections of the family name.

Parents can do so by encouraging their children to work outside the business first—a big recommendation of mine—and earn credibility where it doesn't matter what your last name is. If children then decide they want to work in the family business, and they qualify for the position, they bring credibility and work experience with them. They should have the opportunity at any job opening for which they are qualified. However, too often unqualified children are hired, or positions are created for them. This will always cause discontent and create resentment with other employees in the business.

When qualified family members are hired it provides them opportunities to demonstrate the passion that's essential for leadership in the company. Passion tends to banish any sense of entitlement. As I have indicated, people develop passion by working at something long enough for it to captivate their attention, activate their imagination, and engage them at the deepest levels of their work. Working also requires facing difficulties and adversities to achieve goals. It's the opposite of entitlement, which seeks to gain something without doing the work to get it. Family members have to work not only to obtain their positions, but then perform well, like every other employee.

All these circumstances reassure employees the owners are not catering to their own families, but are putting the best interests of the business first. Family members earn the right to lead by working harder than the employees, and by holding themselves accountable to the same objective standards that measure performance. Those standards include supervision by non-family members who are given the authority to mentor and evaluate family members just as they would any other employees in their charge. This ensures the evaluations are truly

║║║║║║║║║║║║║║║║║║║║║║║║║║║║║║║║║

The best way to earn the right to work
in the family business is by first working
up to a supervisory position
in another company.

║║║║║║║║║║║║║║║║║║║║║║║║║║║║║║║║║

based on results of their performances.

Especially important for family members is advancing in the company based on what they do, not who they are. It's about the work. This maintains the integrity of the business and assures employees both they and their work are valued. Objective performance evaluations also help the family members determine whether or not they have the aptitude and the desire to work in the business. Evaluations can either legitimize their rise to leadership, or help family members realize they would rather do something else with their lives, which releases them to fulfill their passion in another direction. I repeatedly see situations where family members are expected to work in the company. They need to be given the right to leave without repercussions from the family.

Rooting Out Entitlement

If entrenched, entitlement can continue to permeate the business culture into the second and third generations. It's difficult to root out. That's why it's critical to catch it early. Perhaps the first step is to be aware parents tend to default to entitlement when dealing with their children. Loving with indulgence, rather than discipline, is the path of least resistance. The children will then carry these expectations into the business, thinking of ways they can benefit from, rather than contribute to, its success. Entitlement is inherently self-centered. It will hurt a family business dependent on cohesion, commitment, and sacrifice. This is why it's so critical family businesses be intentional about preventing it in the first place.

Preventing entitlement begins by instilling a sense of responsibility for the business in the next generation, starting when the next generation is young. It's important to tell them about the company, what it means to the family, employees, and the community. Begin to involve children in the business in small ways, by giving them part-time jobs so they begin to get a feel for the business, and learn to care about it. Most importantly, being involved teaches them the value of hard work. They will be proud of their contributions. Lay down the ground rules for working in the business, so they understand a position in or ownership of the business is not a guarantee after they graduate from college. They don't have a right to work in the family business. It's a privilege they need to earn. Here's my advice: the best way to earn the right to work in the family business is by first working up to a supervisory position in another company.

Actually, every chapter of this book is about rooting out entitlement. Holding family meetings, forming an outside board, developing passion, working out a long-term transition based on fairness, and developing a strategic plan, are all intentional ways to reverse the effects of entitlement and redirect family energy and talent into the business.

CHAPTER 10

Fair but Not Equal

An interview with a client's daughter-in-law revealed the underlying problem which deals with fairness. "I want my in-laws to realize they have more than one son, and he matters," she said. "I have heard my husband pray the same words every day when he wakes, 'God please help me become as successful as my dad has made my brother.'"

Her husband's parents consistently overlooked him and his brother in favor of their other son. She described the opportunities extended to the favored son—including sole ownership of the family business. She then gave this warning, "If the hurt feelings and resentments for being treated unfairly can't be addressed and resolved…once the favored son is allowed to buy the company, the family will fall apart." Incredulously, she adds, "How could a mother or father not realize the unfairness?"

After this blatant unfairness was brought out in the open during the family meeting, they agreed to establish a hiring policy for the company. Once the younger son obtained experience and qualified for a position in the company, he could be hired and given the opportunity to buy a percentage of the stock.

Life isn't fair, yet we have an innate sense of fairness, and we expect it, especially among family. It's why fairness in a family business is so important. Even if parents have a favorite child, they must work hard at not showing favoritism by being fair to all their children. Being fair can mean the difference between failure or success in business, and discord or unity within the family.

Fair practice in business compares to fair play in sports. Without it, the game degenerates into chaos. In a family business, fairness is a critical component of both the business culture and a successful transition plan, even though that can be challenging. Being fair to all requires wisdom and an understanding of what's best for each family member and the business. Family members might have differing viewpoints on what's fair, especially if some opt to leave the family business, while others stay. Parents often want to divide their estate equally among the children, as if the business were a pie, with each of the children getting the same-sized piece. The instinct that tends to drive parental decisions is not fairness, but equality, which can end up being unfair.

Equal Isn't Fair

When family business owners tell me they want to treat their children equally, I tell them I understand their intent. In reality, though, trying to treat their children equally is not just unwise and naïve, it's impossible. Say, for instance, an owner has four children. Two work in the business, and two don't. In an attempt to treat their children equally, an equal number

The instinct that tends to drive parental decisions is not fairness, but equality, which can end up being unfair.

of shares is given to each of the children. The ones who don't work in the company receive the same amount as those who do. When it comes to distribution of the shares only, that's equal. But it's only truly equal if everything else is equal and if other factors or circumstances remain the same. Yet, in this situation that is clearly not the case. Two siblings who are outside the company have opportunity for success in their chosen careers. The two inside need the same opportunity to build their own careers within the family business, rather than feel like they are employees of their siblings.

It's worth repeating, shares given to family members outside the company will always lead to conflict among the siblings. The family members outside will want to leverage their shares into a position of power. They want to have a say in how the company is run. This is not fair to the ones inside who actually have to carry the burden of running the business and making sure it grows, stays profitable, and continues to benefit the entire family.

When the company is profitable, resentment can build among the insiders, who feel they are working for their siblings on the outside. Conversely, if the company is losing money, the siblings on the outside lose wealth but have their own careers. The insider siblings, who have taken the risk of running the company, have everything to lose, which makes the case for not giving equal shares to outsiders and insiders.

Fairness, unlike equality, can be expressed in different ways depending on the relationship each member of the next generation has to the business. For the siblings who want to stay in the family business, it might mean the older generation selling stock to them at a discount, so they are not saddled by an excessive amount of debt from the start. That same discount needs to be applied to the siblings on the outside in other ways, such as cash, life insurance policies, or other assets of the older generation. This is fair to both, and gives all siblings an opportunity to succeed in their chosen careers.

A Fair Shake

Fairness is fundamental in any business, whether or not it is family-owned. Many studies have determined that concerns about fairness are economically significant. Employers who violate rules of fairness are punished by reduced productivity. When people feel hurt, they tend to retaliate.

On the positive side of the ledger, fairness in companies not only can minimize costs, but can also help increase value. It inspires operational managers to carry out a well-founded strategic plan, or embrace an organizational change.

The act of fairness tells people they matter. Even more, it encourages them to respond positively, to do something with what they have received. It does not guarantee success, but it does help create opportunities for success.

The goal of fairness is to ensure the transition plan has

provided the opportunity to the entire family to parlay the success of the family business into individual fulfillment and success.

This is why fairness is a vital component of a transition plan. When the first generation creates a plan based on fairness, they will think strategically about the future of the company. Fairness prompts them to consider who among the family has the passion and the entrepreneurial savvy to run the business, and will most benefit from owning it. It also means the older generation will think of ways to contribute assets other than stock to the family members who want to pursue other interests.

Alternatively, when fairness is not a consideration, with no fair process in place, it usually indicates the older generation has not engaged in any kind of strategic plan. They have not established family meetings or a family council, during which all family members have a voice and become a part of the transition process. Instead, they simply decide to let "the kids fight over it," which generally dooms the business and creates havoc in the family. Worse, they favor one child to the exclusion of the others who may never get a chance to work in the company. They have "sown the wind," and even if the business manages to survive its founders, it rarely extends beyond the third generation, who have "reaped the whirlwind." When the business falls apart, it's the third generation that often—and unfairly—gets the blame.

Much has been written about how the third generation causes a family business to fail. In my observation, it is the first generation's lack of planning which leads to failure by the third generation. The second generation, taking over a company with no strategic plan, usually can operate that company

|||||||||||||||||||||||||||||||||||||||||||||||

*In my observation, it is the first
generation's lack of planning which leads
to failure by the third generation.*

|||||||||||||||||||||||||||||||||||||||||||||||

successfully in their lifetime. It's when the third generation takes over that it fails, because they've not been taught to think strategically. Also, often by this time the shares have become too widely held and the company struggles to support the increasing number of family members.

With Fairness for All

Fair practice in a family business means that fairness extends throughout the entire company. Hiring and promotion policies are based on aptitude, ability, and performance. This presumes owners and managers have a good understanding of their employees and don't allow favoritism to influence personnel decisions. Family members who work in the business are employees first, family second. They are subject to the same standards, evaluations, and performance reviews as everyone else. To retain objectivity, family members should not be evaluated by other family members, and the evaluations should be based on results. This demonstrates fairness, which engenders trust and loyalty among all family members, as well as employees, ensuring no one receives preferential treatment.

Fairness incorporates values such as hard work, respect, and dignity, to which anyone can aspire and for which anyone can be rewarded. Frequently, though, the hiring practice dictates selecting the smartest recruit. Fairness does not cater to genius when genius thinks it deserves special treatment.

For example, when I was at Arthur Andersen a brilliant young recruit sailed through the entire interviewing process. He was a sure bet to be hired, but we wanted to get a final assessment from the first- and second-year people with whom he'd be working. Two of them took him to lunch, and afterward one came into my office and said, "Les, I know you are high on this guy, and I don't want to hurt his chances, but he wouldn't even talk with us. He didn't want to deal with people at our level."

"Then he's gone," I said. "Seeing his true personality is exactly why we wanted him to have lunch with you."

The poet William Carlos Williams wrote, "Smart ain't necessarily good," and in the work force, smart can be corrosive if it lacks humility, empathy, human kindness, and the willingness to be a team player.

Many Ways of Being Fair

Sometimes a family cannot retain its business and have everyone in the family continue to benefit from it. Sometimes the right and fair thing to do is to sell the business and not transition it to the next generation. As I said before, I always considered selling the business to be an unfortunate outcome until my mentor Lèon Danco told me, "Les, you got them to do *something*." That's the point. When the best option is to sell the business, a family is often reluctant, and sometimes immobilized. They don't want to let go, even when they should.

I worked with one family business which underwent an enormous growth spurt. When the family bought the company, it had $20 million in sales. In less than two decades sales were close to $500 million. The company had grown so fast the first generation was not able to prepare the second generation to run the business. They simply didn't have the experience, expertise, or the passion. For the sake of the family, the first generation decided to sell the company and distribute part of the cash to their children and to the employees. It was a fair outcome for all.

Contrast this to one of the largest family businesses in the United States in terms of revenue. The family members decided they wanted to own the company, as shareholders, but not work in it. The descendants of the founder own over ninety percent of the company shares, and reinvest the company's own earnings to continue to stimulate growth.

One company sold, one company did not. Both were being fair to all the family members, as well as the employees.

Learn to be Fair

We all have a sense of fairness, but also an instinct to be selfish, which inhibits our ability to be fair. It takes discipline to nurture a sense of fairness in our everyday lives and practice it with our family and employees.

Another owner of a family business told me this story: "Early in my career I took a seminar on business management. I have learned since then if you want to help people, you need to be a fair manager. But I didn't understand this at that time. At the end of the seminar, the instructor asked each of us to evaluate the others in the class. One woman stood up and addressed me personally, 'Do you know what your biggest problem is? You don't like people.' I angrily insisted it wasn't true, but I knew she was right. At work, I was a dictator. That was the day I started to change the way I treated people."

That also was the trigger which helped change how he dealt with employees. Over the next fifteen years his company achieved phenomenal growth.

Business owners can be hard drivers, but being fair sometimes means they have to let others drive.

CHAPTER 11

Fire Fast,
Hire Slow

Your people are your most important resource. Your product or service is not the company. Your people are, and the success of your company depends on their performance.

Hiring employees who will build the business and firing those who are no longer contributing to its growth are the two most important tasks of management. If you don't have the right people at the right time, your company will not succeed.

Two questions dominate the process of hiring and firing: who are you bringing in, and when do you let them go? The basic concept safeguarding this process—and the only way to do it well—is to fire fast and hire slow. When done correctly, the positive impact on a company is huge. If you do the opposite—fire slow and hire fast—the negative impact will be just as huge.

This applies to all companies, not just companies in transition. But a company in transition will want to incorporate good

||||||||||||||||||||||||||||||||||||||||||||

As a leader, I got what I tolerated.

||||||||||||||||||||||||||||||||||||||||||||

hiring and firing practices as part of the transition plan, when things are in flux. Good employees will help with a smooth transition, so the next generation can continue to build on what the previous generation has done.

Fire Fast

Firing fast is a simple concept, as are many of the ideas in this book, but hard to do for two reasons. Number one, entrepreneurs never want to let long-term employees go, especially if they are in top management and have helped build the company. Next to letting go of leadership of the company, firing long-standing and faithful employees is the perhaps the hardest thing an owner can do. Owners have developed a relationship with these pioneers, centered around the work they have done together, and to tell them they can no longer work for the company feels like a betrayal.

Secondly, entrepreneurs tend to be overly optimistic about an underperforming employee's ability to change. The vast majority of owners with whom I have worked believe that employees no longer doing a good job will transform themselves into high performers. And they believe they can help that person change. They spend months, and even years, waiting to see it happen, believing it will eventually. But it never does.

That was one of my mistakes when I got to the management

level at Arthur Andersen. I thought I could change people and put them on a performance plan that sometimes lasted far too long and accomplished nothing. When I finally fired a non-achiever, other employees responded, "Why did it take you so long?" As a leader, I got what I tolerated.

When to Fire

How do you know when to fire someone? The short answer is when the company has outgrown them. You will see it before they do, and certainly before they acknowledge they are no longer keeping up with the company's growth. Helping an employee move on, if done well, can be an act of empathy. Fairness is paramount. Treating an exiting employee fairly includes providing a severance agreement, with two to three years of payments, on the condition they do not damage the company's reputation.

Firing employees has a potential upside, if it releases them to find a job to which they are more suited and will find more fulfilling. They will be happier, and as the adage goes, a happy worker is a productive worker.

Hire Slow

Quick hiring can be just as detrimental to a company as slow firing. Hiring too fast tends to happen when management wants to quickly fill a position rather than look for the right person. You might find many immediate candidates for a position but the right person takes much longer to assess.

Hiring the right person means you are looking not just for their qualifications and experience. You are also looking for the intangibles like personality, curiosity, and a willingness to

||||||||||||||||||||||||||||||||||||||||||

One of the keys to that success
was hire for attitude, and train for skills.

||||||||||||||||||||||||||||||||||||||||||

learn. If you are looking to hire the right person, ask yourself, "What's the behavior I want? What kind of attitude does this person have?"

Attitude is everything. Many people have the right skills, but not the right attitude. Herb Kelleher, the chairman of the board of Southwest Airlines, transformed the airline from three jets into the country's largest low-fare carrier, with over 40 straight years of profitability. One of the keys to that success was hire for attitude, and train for skills. "We can train people," he said, "but we can't change their DNA."

As I have noted, entrepreneurs hang on to people too long, believing they will change. They think, "attitude is lacking but the skills are there. We'll change their attitude." That won't happen. Attitudes are ingrained. Skills are learned. A person with the right attitude is far more likely to learn the right skills. If you don't hire for attitude you will soon be firing for attitude, an enormous cost in time, resources and money.

Happy Employees

Hiring is all about filling your company with people who are happy in their work, and know how to have fun that comes from good attitudes and a friendly atmosphere. Work hard at creating an environment where you continue to promote those positive attitudes. Make the work environment enjoyable and watch your employees achieve, and even exceed, their goals.

I once told my management team that having fun was the missing ingredient in our company. "We need to do a fun activity together at least once a week," I said. A member of the team approached me afterwards and said, "Les, I don't understand what that means."

"If you don't know what that means, I shouldn't need to explain it to you. Go find out for yourself." He couldn't, and a year later he was gone.

If you hire for attitude, creating an environment where people with good attitudes can thrive, you will both hire and fire less. You will attract good people eager to work for you and wanting to stay with you. That's how your company will succeed.

CHAPTER 12

Establishing a Family Office

C aring for the family's needs is essential for a smooth transition. The family office can help facilitate a good transition because it will help ensure the family's personal and financial objectives are being met.

The duties of a family office involve more than managing wealth. They also include helping the family identify goals, articulate core values, and pursue strong family relationships. The people hired in your family office will be your most trusted advisers. They will know more about your family and your needs than any outside adviser. The entire family, including in-laws, will have access to these family office advisers.

Think Needs before Costs

Still, many businesses don't see the need for a family office, often because they don't understand how it can make their families' lives much less complicated. They only consider the cost, and view the family office as an added expense, especially if they have recently come into wealth. "Why use our wealth to pay people to manage it?" they ask. This is narrow-minded thinking. Initially, families should be focusing on their needs, not only the costs, which are often less than hiring outside advisers to do everything the family offices can provide. In other words, a family office can save you money. It should not be viewed as an additional expense. However, you will need to determine how to pay for the office with advice from your outside accountants to ensure these payments will be tax deductible.

How much family wealth is necessary to set up a family office? Many advisers disagree on this. Some think the family should have at least one hundred million dollars to justify the costs of a family office. In my opinion, this decision depends on the needs of the family, not the amount of wealth. A family with much less wealth may have certain needs which are important enough to warrant a family office.

Steps for Setting Up a Family Office

If you have decided you need a family office, where do you start? First, make sure you have a strategic plan in place. Setting up a family office without a plan will simply waste your resources.

Secondly, hire a president who has financial experience and may have already worked with the family in an advisory capacity. The entire family needs to fully trust this person and be in complete agreement on their choice. Next to trust, the most important criteria for selecting your president is the ability to hire a skilled staff willing to provide services to your family.

This president should be someone who can help you work through the questions concerning how to manage your wealth, as well as how to pass it on to the next generation. Your family

|||||||||||||||||||||||||||||||||||||||||||||||

The people hired in your family office will be your most trusted advisers. They will know more about your family and your needs than any outside adviser.

|||||||||||||||||||||||||||||||||||||||||||||||

must be the president's number one priority. Both the family and the president need to understand that it's never only about the money. It's about the good you want your wealth to do for your family, the community, or any other areas in which you want to make a difference. In addition, your wealth gives your family many opportunities to enjoy time together and enjoy each other.

The president can also protect your assets and will be the family's first line of defense from people asking for money. As an example, a man came to the family office requesting money for his struggling company. I asked him for his personal balance sheet, which he brought the next day. Immediately I noticed a line item which showed his home valued at nearly a million dollars, with no mortgage. I suggested he take out the largest mortgage possible on his home, and invest it in his company before he ever asked this family office for money. He was not happy with my answer and left the office. About two years later I saw him again. I knew I had given him the right advice when he told me putting his own money at risk had made his company more successful. Because it was his own money, he felt more responsible. I learned to be protective of the family when inundated with many such requests. If I thought requests were valid I would discuss them with the owners or the board to determine if we were interested in loaning the money or making a capital investment.

After hiring a president, the next important decision is where to locate the family office. It should be at a separate, discreet site to prevent people from coming to the door, interrupting, and asking for money. The family office will become a safe place for family meetings and any type of family discussion. It will also provide space where anyone in the family can come to think and plan, with access to family office employees for their advice.

Services a Family Office Can Provide

The following is a list of possible services, not all-inclusive or in any order of importance, your family office can provide:

• **Consulting:** People have asked me if I spent most of my time in the family office overseeing the family's investments. They were always surprised when I told them I only spent about five percent of my time dealing with investments. We hired an outside investment firm which freed me to spend most of my time consulting with individual family members as they learned to live with their wealth. This included advising about business and numerous personal issues which covered starting, buying, or investing in a business; deciding how the children would learn to deal with wealth; building homes; and focusing on sibling relationships.

• **Setting up an outside board:** (see chapter 5) When I was hired to set up a family office, I was asked what I would do first. "Set up an outside board," I said. I had learned from all the companies I had worked with the value and necessity of receiving the kind of independent thought an outside board could provide.

• **Preparation of quarterly financial statements for all family units.** This is very important, especially for those who need to learn how to read and understand these statements.

• **Tax return preparation for the families.** Some family offices have their accounting firms prepare returns. Alternatively, the family office accounting staff can prepare the returns and have the outside accounting firm review them. The office personnel in charge of the financial statements and the tax returns should be CPA's.

• **Bill paying.** Be careful with this. If you pay the bills for younger generations, it might hinder them from being responsible with their money and keeping track of how they are spending their wealth. Older generations, on the other hand, are appreciative of this service because over the years they have been paying their own bills and they understand how their wealth has been managed.

• **Overseeing investments.** While you will undoubtedly rely on the help of a wealth advisory firm, you will also need an internal investment adviser to ensure your investment strategy, including asset allocation and periodic rebalancing, is being followed.

• **Hiring household help for various individuals.**

• **Hiring a human resource person or persons.** This position is often overlooked, not only in family offices but also in family businesses. The head of the HR department should be at the same level as your other top management team members.

• **Helping the family decide if not-for-profits should be** established when the family chooses their commitments to help others.

• **Hiring IT personnel.** Because the tech world changes so rapidly it's crucial to fill these positions.

• **Overseeing private equities.** This is valuable if your family office decides to invest in private companies which are not managed by a money manager. The president and the family office employees will perform due diligence on the companies, with the ability and responsibility to say yes or no to investment decisions.

• **Provide initial advice on contents of wills, powers of attorney, non-compete agreements, pre-nuptial agreements and similar legal issues.** The documents must be drafted by an attorney.

Some of these services could be outsourced. The president, along with the family, will make these decisions. Once you determine the types of services needed you will have the roadmap for hiring. You will decide what type of people you want, as well as the experience these individuals will need for providing the services your family requires.

People ask me how many employees a family office should have. This will again depend on your needs. I have seen a range of one employee up to three hundred. The latter was for a family who owned real estate around the world and needed a large staff to support these locations. Most offices I know range from ten to thirty employees.

Focusing on caring for the family and growing the family's wealth are the main reasons for a family office. Helping the family learn to live with their wealth is equally important.

As you do your strategic planning, I suggest you ask the

question, "What would happen if we didn't set up a family office?" Then work through that scenario to see what your answers are. When deciding about a family office always remember, "Structure follows strategy."

CHAPTER 13

Establishing a Family Council

The greatest challenge of wealth is not how to make it but how to manage it and put it to good use. Dealing with this challenge needs to be included in the transition plan. Wealth is a blessing which carries the burden of responsibility for families who leverage their wealth not only to their benefit but also for the community. In the process of creating a transition plan, keep in mind family business wealth can make or break the family. The results of this make-or-break situation depend on the tools the family uses. A Family Council is one of these vital tools. It can help keep the family together and can mold plans for future transitions.

In most cases a Family Council is the continuation of family meetings, with the entire family included. The major difference is the family members will run the Family Council meetings instead of having a facilitator. However, I recommend the facilitator of the family meetings be present, in an advisory capacity only.

The focus of the Family Council is governance. Simply defined, governance is the way a family manages and grows its wealth, sets policy, as well as strengthens the commitment of the family to stay together. A Family Council also needs to plan family gatherings that include time for fun.

Because family unity is so important, Family Councils should be formed as soon as possible. The size of the company and whether or not the business has been sold or the family still has ownership, should not factor in the decision. What matters is having a dedicated source of guidance from the family. A Family Council manages with one hand on the rudder of values guiding the business and the family, and the other hand giving direction on increasing the family's wealth.

I worked with the owner of a large company whose goal was simple: that the family always stays together. "We don't own our money," he told me. "We are only its caretakers. Our family's responsibility is to manage it well. If we do that, it helps not only our family, but reaches well beyond us." The most satisfying day of the owner's business career was when the sale of the company was finalized, and a very generous share of the proceeds was given both to the employees and the community. As soon as the family business was sold a Family Council was formed. It was given the task of setting up policies to keep the family together, overseeing the management of the wealth, and hiring outside advisers when additional guidance was needed.

Guidance is vitally important. Entrepreneurs are not necessarily good at managing money. Business savvy does not always carry over into fiscal discipline. While entrepreneurs focus on top line growth, they need someone watching the bottom line. This becomes especially important if the business has been sold. Succeeding generations inheriting the wealth from the sale should have been taught to appreciate the hard work and discipline it took to accumulate that wealth, and not allow it to depreciate in value.

More Than the Money

Ask family business founders why they started their companies. I know what the answer *won't* be: "I wanted to get rich." First, they have ideas and can visualize them as realities. Their satisfaction comes from using their entrepreneurial talents to improve their families, their communities, and their world by developing their ideas. Along with this is the understanding their companies have larger obligations to society which go beyond profits. Wealth is not the goal; it is a byproduct.

Family members can't appreciate the value of wealth until they first absorb the values that generated the wealth, such as hard work, pride in work well done, ingenuity, sacrifice, creating opportunities for others, and civic responsibility. Values determine the extent to which people, whether entrepreneurs, or employees in established businesses, pour their energies into a business. The resulting wealth from such industrious efforts continues to support the values. A Family Council can then oversee the wealth so it continues to benefit the family and society.

Failure to Understand Wealth

The following true story shows what can happen when family members don't appreciate how they obtained their wealth. The head of a Family Council opened every meeting with this

||||||||||||||||||||||||||||||||||||||||||||

In the process of creating a transition plan, keep in mind that family business wealth can make or break the family.

||||||||||||||||||||||||||||||||||||||||||||

warning, "If you continue spending at this rate you will run out of money!" The family always gave the same response, "The checks have always come in." During one meeting the Family Council leader said, "We're at the point where you're going to have to start paying attention to the utility bills!" They responded in astonishment, "We have to pay for utilities?" This extreme example demonstrates the drastic disconnect between the illusion of a lifestyle of wealth and the reality of the real world.

In this case, the family did run out of money. It was due to the failure of the Family Council, which had instructed the office personnel to automatically pay all expenses for each of the family members. They had ignored the "five percent rule", recommended by family offices and good advisers, which states if you spend more than five percent of your wealth you will eventually deplete it. Without a spending policy this particular family went well beyond the "five percent" and did end up depleting their wealth.

The numerous inheritors of family wealth are often unprepared to handle it. I have always recommended bill payments be made for the oldest generation, but following generations make their own payments so they understand where their money is being spent.

If succeeding generations don't understand the value of wealth and the hard work required to earn it, they will spend it without any thought of how they received it. Inheriting a windfall can cause some to decide they don't need to work, and if that happens chances are the money will be squandered.

The Value of Work

Work is what entrepreneurs dream about and live for. Our country is based on democracy and built on the hard work of generations free to choose or create their employment and run their own businesses. A socialist government cannot provide the same opportunity because it devalues work. Government ownership destroys production and the incentive to work. To work is to take pride in creating goods and providing services important to society. A job is more than a means to an end. It constitutes part of a worker's identity. Work is meaningful, contributing to an economy that not only creates wealth, but also brings other benefits to a society. An example of this are the many foundations that have been established by families of wealth.

Part of the work of the Family Council is to keep emphasizing the value of work to the family members. The younger generations should be taught to appreciate the hard work of members of their older generations. If the family still owns the business, a Family Council can establish policies to prevent entitlement, such as the five-year rule: any family members who want to work in the family business must first work five years outside the company. After that time, they can then only be hired in the family business if there's a position for which they qualify. To simplify: the business should not create a position for a family member.

The value of work reinforces the value of money. If succeeding generations have absorbed the first-generation work ethic, they will more readily take the Family Council's advice on how to handle the family wealth. Many families determine how the wealth is passed down, attaching conditions to its distribution. Others put the money in trusts, dictating how much can be withdrawn and how the money is to be spent. Families with immense wealth, like the Rockefellers, set up trusts in perpetuity to be distributed to six or seven generations into the future. These trusts can also help alleviate the tax burden. Warren Buffet has earmarked most of his estate for charity, leaving considerably less for his children, in keeping with his personal philosophy that "a very rich person should leave his kids enough to do anything, but not enough to do nothing."

Stigma of Wealth

The Family Council can also help the family deal with the stigma of wealth. People tend to resent the wealthy simply because of envy. A business owner I worked with was attending a city council meeting when someone stood up, called him by name, and said, "He owes us. He got rich off of us!" Such comments are misguided and irresponsible, showing ignorance of the facts.

The business owner had employed hundreds of people in the city. Like most family business owners, this owner valued the employees and treated them accordingly, through training and by incentivizing them to work hard. The business provided a product benefitting millions of families throughout the country and pumped billions of dollars into the economy.

Children can also suffer the stigma of wealth when they feel picked on and excluded by their peers. It's not uncommon for a child of a wealthy family to be subjected to comments like, "Why don't you just ask your grandparents for the money?" Or, "Your grandparents could buy that for our school." Situations like this are very hard for these children to face. The Family Council can ensure policies are in place to help train the children how to respond if this happens to them.

People know the family is wealthy, but often don't understand that it's not unusual for a family's wealth to be tied up in trust or invested in other non-liquid assets. This could mean cash is not readily available, especially to the underage children, but frequently for their parents as well.

Following are some guidelines for formation of the Family Council Leadership Team:

- Membership on the Family Council Leadership Team is a privilege, not a burden, because it is a proven way to keep the family together.
- Members are chosen by the entire family.
- Membership includes representatives age twenty-one or over from each generation, including the in-laws, and should have a fair ratio of females and males.
- Suggested membership should be at least five, but not exceed nine.
- Chairperson is chosen by Leadership Team members.
- Term limits are the same as being a board member, not to exceed ten years.

Responsibilities of the Leadership Team include:

- Meet no more than twice a year and schedule a year in advance.
- Create agendas for upcoming Family Council meetings, including information from anyone, other than family members, who will be reporting at these meetings.
- Bring in outside advisers, if needed, to help resolve current issues.

Following is an example of what an agenda for a Family Council meeting may include:

MORNING

- Report from president of the company if the family still has ownership
- Report from president of the Family Office
- Report from president of the Family Foundation
- Closed session—excuse presidents of above entities
- Discuss ways to teach the youngest generation about the family's wealth
- Discuss additional questions and/or issues

LUNCH

AFTERNOON

- Tour a museum
- Go to a park to play

You may find the last items surprising, but there is a reason I include them. I was on the advisory board of a large bank where the meetings included numerous heads of family offices. One particular concern was brought up repeatedly: Family

Council meetings were scheduled too often, the agendas were too long, and they were all about business. They included no recreational activities, getting together just for the fun of it. "All work and no play" is not healthy, and runs the risk of "burning out" many family members, which will destroy the value of the meetings. This is why I recommend only two Family Council meetings per year. Any more than that and the meetings will feel like a burden, rather than a privilege.

CHAPTER 14

Why You Need a Buy-Sell Agreement

"**Y**ou can't do that to me!"

"We have to," I replied. "It's what you agreed to do."

It was also what I had insisted on: the inclusion of a clause stipulating a buyout in the event of a disability.

The company president had just suffered a debilitating stroke. He now had to face a buyout of his shares at a discount, as stipulated by the buy-sell agreement he had put in place just months prior.

The president had set up the buy-sell to protect the business, which was owned by five non-family members. Still in his fifties, he did not expect to be the one relinquishing ownership.

"What if this had happened to one of the other owners?" I asked.

"It would have triggered the buy-sell," he acknowledged, "just as it did to me." The buy-sell had functioned as intended, an integral part of a larger plan protecting the business from an unforeseen catastrophic event.

Protect Your Future

This book is about planning for the future of the business, its transition to succeeding generations, the well-being of the family, and life after letting go. These plans need protection against what we can anticipate but can't control, like death or a debilitating occurrence. A buy-sell agreement provides needed protection for family and closely-held businesses. It acknowledges we don't know what's going to happen, but we can prepare for the unforeseeable.

I worked with the husband and wife who owned a company and had given stock equally to their three children. Two of the children worked in the company and I raised the question, "Can a child who does not work in the company be bought out?" Because they had no buy-sell agreement in place, the family could not figure out a fair price for the stock. This quandary often leads to an impasse. The child outside the company doesn't think the buy-out price is high enough, while those working in the company think it's too high.

I compare a buy-sell to a marriage contract which includes a divorce agreement. It seems cynical, but it acknowledges a statistical reality. Nobody plans for a divorce, but everyone can prepare for the possibility. Business owners don't want to think of what might happen when someone leaves the company. They don't want to talk about it. I often hear, "We'll cross that bridge when we get there." When they get to the bridge, they pay dearly for crossing it, and regret they had not put a buy-sell in place. It's the price businesses pay for not thinking long term.

To further illustrate the value of a buy-sell, I worked with a client whose friend invested several hundred thousand dollars in the client's company, in exchange for three percent of the stock. The friend was certain the company would do well, and my client was grateful for the infusion of cash. Years passed and the company grew. The friend wanted to collect, demanding an outrageous amount of money. A buy-sell had never been put in place. After a bitter dispute, my client agreed to the price. The friend had become a liability to the company. and they needed him out. The founders had naively assumed they did not need a buy-sell agreement, and paid the price for their mistake.

Terms of a Buy-Sell

Owners of closely-held businesses should enter into buy-sell agreements for their ownership interests. A buy-sell removes the stress if business owners part ways because all shareholders had agreed to the terms when the buy-sell was drafted. A proper value is established based on an evaluation of the company and an attached discount. The price is set per the agreement, and varies year to year as determined by a fluctuating valuation formula. This keeps the agreement price from getting stale and also assures both parties agree to the price of the buyout.

It is important to keep in mind, however, the primary objective of a buy-sell is the protection of the long-term interests of the company. A good practice is to take out a life insurance policy on each person who has ownership in the company and make either the company or individuals its beneficiaries. Upon the death or disability of an owner, the company can then buy the stock back, or family members buy the stock, without causing financial strain. Because real life has a way of trumping the best plans, the buy-out needs to be flexible enough to accommodate different scenarios to protect the company. For example, a buy-out can be immediate, or paid out over a term of five to ten years. There also could be a pre-payment clause, depending on how well a company is doing, what it can afford at the time, and its cash flow situation.

I indicated at the beginning of this chapter, the importance of defining and including in the buy-sell agreement what happens if a shareholder is disabled. I have seen too many of these agreements focus only on the death of a shareholder. Make sure a doctor has written the definition of disability in the document. Usually, these definitions will indicate whether the disabled will be able to perform their duties as they did prior to the disability. This statement will make it clear whether the buy-out is triggered, and reduce, to a great extent, the questioning by the disabled shareholder or the family.

T hank you for reading my book! I really hope it has giv-en you alternative ideas to consider prior to establish-ing your transition plan.

Some books you read and set aside. When you come to the last page you know how the story ends. By reading this book, you know it's not a story. Your family and your business are the story and this book is a guide. You can refer to any chapter to apply practical ideas as you continue to write the story of your family business.

One of my goals, after you've read this book, is that you will not avoid having family meetings. I know this was stressed in the book and I know it's not easy to do, but I want to make sure you understand the critical importance of a facilitated family meeting.

Time is a gift. Don't wait for things to happen to your business. Get to know what you don't know. Apply the practical solutions. Learn to speak by listening first. Learn to make decisions based on what you've learned from listening, especially to your advisers and board members. Be open to the idea of letting go and allowing others who are passionate about your company to continue what you've begun.

Years ago I held a seminar, "Sixteen Common Mistakes in

Owning and Transitioning a Business." At the end of my presentation someone commented, "One of those sixteen really hit home. We're going to start to fix it today!" Another person asked, "What if all sixteen are an issue?" That got a laugh from the crowd, but I knew it was a serious question. It can be overwhelming if an owner needs to work on everything. Remember to refer to the issues and answers in this book for advice, taking one issue at a time.

Thank you, again, for "listening."

ACKNOWLEDGMENTS

W riting this book has been very gratifying. That's because it's about so many good people I have worked with for over forty years. I have gained as much from you as I have given. Thank you.

Leon Dánco was the first to introduce me to the many issues a family-owned company faces. Dett Hunter taught me the value of thinking strategically. Clay Mathile, former owner of The Iams Company, gave me many ideas on how a company should be run. Dave Sullivan has teamed with me during strategic planning sessions for a number of my clients.

I could not have written my book without the help of my wife, Kathy. Together we carefully edited the entire manuscript, with Kathy making sure you hear my voice when you're reading the book. I also could not have written this book without Rob Lewis of Kite Glass Writing. He helped me distill a great deal of information and experience. It is my intention you will find this book to be a practical resource. Thanks also to Dave Goetz and Melissa Parks of CZ Strategy for their assistance in shaping the book.

Made in the USA
Monee, IL
29 March 2021